HEALING

A Story of Courage

NICOLE DALBY

First paperback edition October 2024

Cover photography by Kait Simek

ISBN (Paperback): 979-8-218-52457-9

This one's for you, Papason.

Note from the Author

I recently attended a four-day meditation retreat, where I had the pleasure of rooming with an incredible soul named Christine. Christine is a transgender woman who made her transition at the age of sixty-one. I am so honored that she chose to share a piece of her life story with me, including the details of why she underwent such a life-altering transformation.

When explaining her transition to me, Christine said, "I didn't want to die with no one ever knowing who I really am."

That one sentence still gives me chills. And I think it encompasses the purpose of this book.

When I wrote my first book, *The Courage to Be You*, my goal was to capture what it meant to me to live an authentic life. I shared some of the life lessons and stories that have led me to become more of who I am and live out my true voice in the world. At the time, it was a basic representation of who I was becoming. It's scary to be vulnerable enough to publish your ideas for others to criticize, and because of that, I feel like I barely dipped my toes into the potential of sharing my authentic self with the world. However, I did it, and I am still really proud of that book. It opened the doors for this second one to come to life in a deeper and greater way.

This book means so much to me. As Christine said, this is my way of sharing who I really am. It's my story, my authentic voice, my journey of heartbreak and healing, and my way of expressing that higher self that calls to each of us when we still our minds and listen. It is vulnerable and messy, but I was reminded recently that a butterfly is most vulnerable after its messy transformation, and the result is a stunning miracle.

In Mark Nepo's *The Book of Awakening*, he shares part of his story of overcoming cancer and what he's learned throughout his journey. His July 1 entry holds the following wisdom about the heart's courage: "It was this honoring of what is true that guided me through my cancer experience: saying no to brain surgery and yes to rib surgery, saying yes to chemo and no to chemo. Each decision appeared both courageous and illogical to my doctors. Since then, I have been called heroic for surviving, which is like championing an eagle for finding its nest, and I have been condemned as selfish for seeking the Truth, which is like blaming a turtle for finding the deep. Courage of this sort is the result of being authentic."[1]

---

1 Material excerpted from *The Book of Awakening* © 2020, 2011, 2000 by Mark Nepo is used with permission from Red Wheel Weiser, LLC Newburyport, MA www.redwhee/weiser.com.

The following chapters are my nest and my deep. They are both miraculous and illogical to many who will read them, and yet, they are simply my story—a story that is calling to be told because it is who I am and this is where the Truth is taking me.

Introduction

The word "trauma" is defined in many different ways by different people. There are small traumas and larger traumas, complex traumas, acute traumas, generational traumas, and secondary traumas. No matter how you categorize or define trauma, every human being has experienced it in one way or another, and everyone has to face the sometimes-daunting and sometimes-joyful task of healing.

I don't believe in a hierarchy of the types of pain we face. Someone grieving the loss of a loved one and someone grieving a job transition are both processing pain in their own way. A new mom experiencing the joy of her baby is also grieving the loss of her independence and the life she used to have. The loss of a pet or a dear friend moving away both come with distinguishing sorrows. And the grief attached to the numerous types of breakups and relationship ends can feel never-ending.

When we step away from the comparisons, the "how-tos" and "shoulds" of how healing may look, we can recognize that every person we meet has a string of challenges to face that they might still carry with them. Healing can be a very isolating experience, and yet, if we each shared our stories, we would see that we do not stand by ourselves on our journeys. Our stories may be different, but we are not alone in trying to process those moments that redefine our lives. I believe it's important to talk about these moments and the harsh reality of what it means to be human some days. Because the less we talk about these feelings and happenings, the more isolated we perceive ourselves to be.

My story is unique, and at the same time, it is no more or less challenging than anyone else's. It has rocked me to my core and changed who I am as a person, and it has reconnected me with the highest life that lives in each of us. I am grateful to be able to share my story in the hopes that it inspires you to find your voice.

As with my first book, my intention is not to tell you how to live your life. I don't claim to write self-help books, because what has worked for me and my journey may differ from what will work for you. I simply hope to share with you my story, the lessons that have come from it, and the path that I've taken so that you may find some inspiration to seek your own path. I hope to empower you to live your most authentic life and to heal in a way that resonates with your soul.

Wherever you are in your journey, you are not alone, and you are so loved.

Thank you for taking the time to read my story. I hold you in love, light, and peace.

Section 1
Love on Fire

I am one of those people who believes that everything happens for a reason—not in the sense that we are powerless to life and, as victims, we must cave to everything that happens, good or bad, but in the sense that everything happens for a reason because we exist for a reason. We came to this earth with a purpose and unique gifts, and the series of events that happen in our lives help us realize and share these gifts if we choose to.

It's the same with the people who come in and out of our lives. Some souls bring us lessons, joy, or guidance. Others bring heartbreak, frustration, and tension. Some may be nothing more than mirrors of how we experience life in that very moment. No matter when or where they come in, I believe that everyone has a purpose in our stories, tiny or great, even when that purpose feels catastrophic.

Chase was one of the big souls in my life story. He brought a little bit of everything and still teaches me things to this day. Our story does not have a happy ending, but my personal story has a happy continuation. It's for that reason that I will never regret the relationship we had or the choices I made with him. I would go back and do it all again, even knowing the things that I do now. My healing journey began and continues because of Chase, and for that, I am grateful. This is our story.

Chapter 1

The Meet-Cute

Chase and I met at work. I was a supervisor at a big-box gym, and he transferred to my location as an assistant manager. I had been there for over two years at the time, and it was pretty common to have a new manager come through. A friend of mine later said that managing fitness professionals is like herding chickens, and the gym where I worked was no different. I heard a lot of talk about Chase from the regional team saying that he was great at what he did and he would make great changes for our location. Having been part of the chicken herding for a couple of years, I didn't have high hopes or expectations.

Nothing about the day I met him was particularly special—he'll tell you that I walked up to him and showed him my "sweet dance moves." (People who know me understand that means I shake my hips and act ridiculous because I like making people laugh.) I'm not sure I did that the moment I met him, but it did come up at some point in the conversation. He was very quiet but pleasant. We talked about what was and wasn't working at the gym, discussed some cleaning tasks, and that was about the extent of our "meet-cute."

Fast-forward a month, and I had come to realize something was different about Chase. He was much more empathetic than other managers I had worked with. I tend to speak about a hundred miles an hour, and I noticed that Chase not only kept up with everything I said to him, but he would act on it. He listened, genuinely cared about what I told him, and made changes accordingly. And this wasn't just for me—this was for every team member he worked with. He managed to gain the trust and loyalty of ninety percent of our team, which wasn't easy. I started to see why the regional team had spoken so highly of him.

We worked together for three months before he quickly got promoted to general manager at another location. I was upset when he told me he was leaving, because I didn't connect as well with our general manager and I didn't think anyone would understand the team like Chase did. He had made some close connections in the short time he'd worked with us, especially with me. I wrote him a letter before he transferred, explaining why I felt so connected to him and thanking him for being such a good person. It was a heartfelt letter, but I didn't expect our relationship to go much further than the gym. I figured we would be the typical "work friends" who stayed in touch for a month before losing interest. Chase had different plans.

After transferring to his new location, Chase invited me out for drinks to tell me about the new job and get caught up on what he was missing with the team. I was happy to see him again and share the latest gym gossip. After about fifteen minutes, however, I realized that Chase's intentions were not just to have drinks as friends. He was there to get to know me in a more personal way. He asked a lot of questions about my past, my family, my interests, and my passions. This went on for a couple of hours before I noticed how late it had gotten.

After I left the bar and got into my car, I couldn't decide how I felt about the whole situation. Chase was a really good guy, and the conversation was easy and carefree. I wouldn't have minded spending more time with him, but I wasn't looking for a relationship, and I didn't see Chase as more than a friend. At the same time, I hadn't connected with someone like that in a long time. He felt like he understood me on so many levels, which was refreshing. It created a strange personal debate in my head.

I made the decision to continue our relationship as just friends for several months because I wasn't ready to start dating. I had recently ended a six-year relationship and wanted to spread my wings and explore before getting attached to someone new. Right after I ended that relationship, I had also come out to my friends and family as queer and had no idea what that looked like yet. And lastly, on top of all that, Chase was going through a divorce after a nine-year marriage resulting in three kids, which seemed like a lot to take on. I wasn't prepared to deal with the numerous obstacles at the time, so I chose the less complicated path.

During those months, Chase was very persistent. He respected my wishes to remain friends, but he was not shy about expressing his desire for more. I watched him go through his divorce and listened whenever he wanted to talk, and he supported me as I transitioned out of a straight and traditional relationship, chopped off my hair, acquired more tattoos, and walked into a more authentic and unstable version of myself. My true views of the world and how I wanted my life to look were changing, and Chase was there to listen and hold space for whatever that looked like.

I suppose we can't choose how love happens. But the more time we spent together, the closer we got. For that, I am grateful, as I believe that everything happens for a reason, and no matter how things ended, I know that we were supposed to be together for the time that we were. He finally broke down my walls (with the help of being quarantined together during COVID-19), and we started a relationship. Beautifully put together and, at the same time, a total train wreck, over the next three years, our partnership became nothing less than a roller coaster on fire.

Chapter 2

The Relationship

Chase and I had an extremely rocky start to our relationship. We had huge low points as well as some of the best moments I had ever spent with anyone. Chase embraced me and my transitions in life like no one else ever had, and I broke down a lot of the walls he had built from his life experiences. Childhood trauma and a short career as a medic had given Chase a rough exterior, and I was one of the few people he talked to about those struggles. This helped us connect in a way that a lot of people didn't understand. Between that and my newfound authenticity, we felt like soulmates. At the same time, however, we had communication flaws that made our relationship unstable.

One agreement I made with Chase before we got together was that I wanted an open relationship. I had started to learn about polyamory, and having just come out as queer, my heart called to explore relationships with more than one person at a time. He agreed, and at first, we had a very healthy understanding and good communication around this topic. I went on dates with other people and could share these experiences with Chase afterward, which helped us grow as a couple.

Then things started to change. Talking to and meeting other people was one thing, however, when I met a woman who I connected with and began to date, the tension between Chase and me became more serious. We argued more about the topic and couldn't find resolutions to our disagreements. It became clear that Chase was not as okay with an open relationship as he had originally indicated. Being new to the experience, I didn't have the tools or words to work through our challenges.

Eventually, the conflict became a nonentity. I fell out of touch with the woman I was seeing, and I didn't meet anyone else I connected with as deeply after that. My conversation with Chase never got resolved, but it also didn't present itself again except in the form of a brief question or two.

We also argued often about how much sex we had. Chase wanted to have more sex than I usually did, but something about the way we argued about it was off. It was almost like we were arguing about two different things—Chase would be upset about the sex, and I would be upset over the way Chase wouldn't listen to my feelings surrounding the argument. Later, I observed this as arguing in a spiral that never came to a point, but at the time, it was frustrating as hell, and neither of us knew how to get past it.

Then we would have disagreements about how involved I should be with Chase's kids and the communication he had with his ex-wife. I knew Chase wasn't telling me every detail of his relationship with her, and to be frank, I didn't push the matter because it didn't feel like my business. I also believed the disagreement around my involvement with his kids was pretty standard for whatever type of mixed-family relationship we had, so it didn't feel important to pursue.

We continued this up-and-down roller coaster for almost two years before things began to shift again. I can't tell you why, to be honest. There wasn't an "aha" moment or a great breakthrough in communication. I don't know if either of us even had any revelations. For some reason, we started to communicate better, not about everything but about certain things, and we grew softer with each other. Maybe we just started to love each other more. The arguments became fewer and farther between, and we flowed into a life together. Whatever it was, we reached a deeper level of trust, openness, and understanding, and from that moment on, we had a relationship that I could only describe as fierce love.

I became more involved with Chase's kids. I had dinner with their family every now and then, and we took the boys on vacation together. Chase opened up to me more about his past and his feelings, and I felt more comfortable making him a priority in my life. He used to be a topic of conversation among my friend group, just like the weather, but now, I was telling my friends how our relationship had grown more serious in many ways. Against everything I'd ever believed about myself, we even talked about having kids of our own. It was a conversation I never thought I would have.

Traveling together became easy, and we were fortunate to visit several national parks. Date night was the highlight of our week, and it felt like we shared everything with each other. It was an unmatched happiness, and I was settling into a life with this man. I had a connection to Chase's soul that I'd never had with anyone before. We understood each other on a different level, and we supported each other through very difficult times.

I guess we did our relationship out of order, but during our last year as a couple, we were in what I would consider the honeymoon phase. It felt like we were on a path toward forever—not the marriage-and-white-picket-fence type of forever, but a forever that worked for us. A forever where we would build a life together and face the world as a team.

However, the only constant in life is change. And my forever changed in an instant, just like many do.

Chapter 3

The Break-in

On December 26, 2022, (three and a half years after Chase and I first met), I was driving back to my apartment from my mom's house in Colorado Springs. I had spent the weekend of Christmas with her and my brother, and Chase had stayed home in my apartment with our cat, Claire. Chase had been living in my apartment with me five days a week for the past year.

Thirty minutes from home, I got a phone call from Chase.

"Love, I don't want you to freak out, but the apartment has been broken into."

Already freaking out, I responded, "What? Are you okay? Is Claire okay? Is anything missing?"

"I'm okay. Claire is fine, but the safe is gone."

I had kept a fifty-pound safe in my closet with everything important in case of a fire or other natural disaster. It contained my social security card, my birth certificate, my passport, the title to my car, etc. It also held my dad's wedding ring from his marriage to my mom and a five-ounce gold bar that my stepdad had gifted to each of the kids a year earlier. If you're like I was when I received the gift and not savvy about the price of gold, at the time, they were each worth close to ten thousand dollars.

"Fuck, fuck, fuck, fuck." I couldn't think past freakout mode.

"I know, I know. I've already called the police, and they are on the way. I'll call you after they leave." Chase was trying to stay as calm as he could.

I hung up the phone, and my mind started whirling. This is one of those things that you hear of happening to other people but never expect it to happen to you. I lived on the third floor of an apartment complex for several reasons—one of which was because it was safer than living on the ground floor. Why would anyone have risked the time and energy to break into a third-story apartment?

Fifteen minutes later, Chase called me back to explain what the police officer had told him.

"The officer took down all our information and gave me a case number. I told him what items were stolen from the safe, and he will type up a report."

"Did he say if he thinks someone broke in or had a key?"

"He checked the lock with his kit, and the lock was definitely picked. He said that we could have changed the locks when we moved in, but it wouldn't have done much in this situation because it's a pretty sturdy lock. They have a lot of break-ins this time of year because people are trying to steal Christmas gifts. He said they've had twenty in this neighborhood in the past week."

Silence. I had no idea what to say.

Chase continued. "The good news is that he said ninety-nine percent of identity theft is done online and not with physical documents anymore. Odds are they will take your valuables and dump your documents with the safe. The police put out a notice to check the surrounding area in case they toss your safe or the documents, and they will alert the pawn shops to watch for the ring and the gold bar."

By this point, I started to process more. "Did they take anything else? What about the money in the Christmas bags on the table or my jewelry or laptop or iPad?"

"The only other thing they took was the fifty dollars in our date-night jar. They didn't touch anything else."

"Okay. I'll be home soon, and we can go to Home Depot to get a security system."

After I hung up again, I called my mom, dad, and brother to tell them what had happened. My brother had recently installed a security system in his home, and I wanted to make sure I had all the information from him so I could get one. Each one of them asked a few questions, but overall, they just made sure that I knew they were there for me if I needed anything.

When I got home, I walked through the apartment

to confirm everything that Chase had said. I'm going to pause here and send my love and care to anyone who's ever experienced theft or a break-in of any kind. It is such a violation of personal space, and it's a feeling I don't ever want to have again. Knowing that someone else has been in your home is gut-wrenching.

We went to Home Depot to buy a Ring security system, though Chase assured me the police officer believed we would not be a target again since the thief already got everything they wanted. I started to install it right away, not wanting to take any chances. I knew I wouldn't feel safe without it.

As I was installing the security system, Chase went to the grocery store to get dinner. Thirty minutes later, he returned home and started pounding on the door like someone was chasing him. This did nothing for my nerves, which were already on high alert, and I opened the door, ready to yell at him for scaring me. When I opened it, he burst in, breathless, with my fifty-pound safe in his hands.

I stood and stared at him in complete shock.

"I had a gut feeling on my way home to drive around the neighborhood, and I'm so glad I did because this was in the field on the corner!" he said between breaths.

I grabbed the mud-covered safe.

"You can see the lock is severely scratched. They must have picked it," Chase said as I opened it.

It was just as the officer had told him it would be. Every

one of my documents was still in the safe, with my dad's ring and the gold bar missing. A wave of relief washed over me. I was devastated to lose my dad's ring, and ten thousand dollars is no small amount of money, but at least I had one less thing to worry about. Everything had happened so quickly, I had no time to think about anything in detail. My documents were safe, the security system was going up, and the police were looking for my valuables. I could breathe again, even if it was just a quarter breath more.

I immediately called my family and shared the good news. My brother came over and brought me wine and flowers to make sure I was okay. We talked about everything for a while, and he gave me a big hug. The rest of the night is a blur. After he left, I finished installing the security system, started researching identity theft, and at some point, fell asleep for what short amount of rest I could find. In a matter of ten hours, my home had been broken into, my possessions stolen and partially returned, and my sense of security stripped. I wish it would have stopped there.

Chapter 4

The Reveal

The week after the break-in was not fun. Trying to sleep in an apartment that someone had burgled was near impossible. Not to mention having to walk out to my car in the dark at 4:30 a.m. to get to work by myself. I was on high alert and watching over my shoulder every time I walked outside. What if someone was still watching my apartment for one of us to leave so they could break in again? How did I know that it wasn't one of my neighbors I saw every day? What if the thief had taken pictures of all my documents and was out there opening bank accounts in my name and creating a new identity?

Society didn't help matters much. Filing for identity theft that hasn't happened yet is near impossible unless someone has, in fact, already used your identity falsely. The man at the bank told me I couldn't do much except file for Equifax, which I did. My barber made sure I knew how unwise it was to keep such important documents and valuables all in a safe in my apartment. My brother kept calling to ask if I had spoken to the police about the case specifics (he was oddly adamant about it). And to top it off, many people I spoke to had me convinced it was someone who worked in my apartment complex because who else could pick the lock and know exactly where my safe was without touching anything else?

To say it was all very overwhelming would be an understatement. I started telling people I didn't want to talk about it anymore and I just wanted to move on. Chase had helped me research identity theft, and I had taken what small steps I could to protect myself going forward. I moved all my valuables to a more secure location, and I came to terms with the fact that I would probably never see my dad's ring or the gold bar again. Eventually, I made it through the week, and things felt like they were calming down a bit.

That Friday, December 30, I coached my regular 5 a.m., 6:10 a.m., and 7:15 a.m. classes at the gym where I worked near downtown. I finished coaching and walked out around 8:30 a.m. to find my dad in the parking lot. He lived thirty minutes from my work without morning rush hour traffic. Seeing him parked outside that early in the morning made my heart drop immediately. What was he doing here? I was ready for him to tell me that someone had passed away or worse.

He did his best to put on a smile, called me "sunshine,"

as usual, and gave me a big hug. Then he said he had something to tell me and asked me to get in his car. Heart pounding, I followed him and prepared for the worst.

"I hate to be the one to tell you this, champ, and I couldn't do it over the phone. Your mom and brother were suspicious about some of the things Chase told you this week. They felt it was strange that he found the safe with all your documents still in it, and your brother said that Chase wouldn't look him in the eye when he was at your apartment on Monday night. They asked me to call the police station to see exactly what the report said about the break-in." He paused for a second. So far, he had done a damn good job of making it sound like a story he would tell me on any other day. Then he continued. "Cole, there is no record of a break-in on file for your address."

I stared at him, blinking for what felt like an hour. "Wait, what?" I finally choked out.

"I don't know if Chase stole the safe or if he's covering for someone else, but for some reason, he lied about filing a police report."

I sat for what felt like an eternity. The world seemed to move in slow motion, and I wasn't catching on, almost like Dad had said something I must not have heard correctly. Did I? "Holy shit." I started shaking.

"Yeah." My dad gave a huge sigh while I sat and processed. Seconds felt like hours that dragged on.

"I don't know what to do," I finally said.

"I want you to know that no matter what you decide, we are all here to support the choice you make, Cole."

"Thanks, Dad."

We sat for a while, just listening to each other breathe. I cried, then I laughed, not knowing what else to do or say. I think my dad would have sat there for hours with me if I'd needed him to.

"I guess I need to drive up to his work and talk to him." It was the only thing I could think of.

"Do you want me to come with you?"

"No, I'm sure that will just make things worse. I'll call you if I need help."

"Okay, I'm here for anything you need."

"Thank you, Dad."

I gave my dad a hug, told him I loved him, and slowly walked to my car. Once I sat, I took a deep breath at the thought of what I was about to do. I think that's when the adrenaline kicked in, and I'm so glad that it did because I went into autopilot. There's no manual for this kind of thing. I knew what had to be done but had no clue how to do it, and yet, something kept me moving forward. The surge of chemicals that floods our bodies in stressful situations sends us into fight-or-flight mode and is meant to keep us safe for a reason. It kept my focus on survival for the next twelve hours.

One thing I will never take for granted is how hard that conversation with my dad had to be for him. I am forever grateful to him for loving me enough to come to me and support me for that moment and for everything else that came next.

Chapter 5

The Crash, the Burn, and the Wreckage

On my way up to Chase's work, my mom called me and asked how I was doing. What was I supposed to say? I was shocked and sad and angry and hopeful that this wasn't actually happening and it was all a mistake that he would have a logical answer for. I had no way to explain what I felt because I couldn't allow the emotion yet. She made a good point that I should probably call the apartment complex and have them change the locks before I got home in case things didn't go well. I did and gave them a basic explanation of what was happening in case Chase showed up.

I've never experienced the phrase "You don't know how strong you truly are until you have to be" until the moment I got to Chase's work. I parked right outside the front door and didn't hesitate to go in and ask to speak with him. Chase followed me out to the sidewalk so his coworkers wouldn't hear the conversation.

I started right in. "I called the police station to see if they found the gold bar yet, and they said there's no report filed for a break-in at my apartment." I didn't want to give him all the details from the morning.

Chase stumbled for a minute, looked shocked, then said, "Wait, so you think I did it?"

My heart sank. His automatically defensive response told me what I had hoped wasn't true.

"I never said that, Chase. All I'm saying is there's no report on file, and I want to know why you lied about it."

"There has to be a report! Of course I filed it. I'll call them and get it."

"Okay, well, until that happens, I'm going to leave your things outside the apartment. The complex has already changed the locks." I started to shake, but I wouldn't leave until the conversation was done.

"So, you are accusing me of doing it! Why would I steal your safe?"

"I don't know, Chase. I hope you can find the police report."

And with that, I drove away.

Adrenaline kept me going, and I got busy as soon as I got home. It took me almost two hours to pack all of Chase's things into boxes and bags. I lined them up outside the front door and texted him that he would need to pick them up by

3 p.m. that day. I was extremely nervous for him to come to the door, but the complex wouldn't let me leave his belongings in the leasing office, and I didn't want to dump them in the parking lot.

I cleaned the apartment while I waited for him to come and get his things. I felt like I had to stay busy. When he got to the front door, he tried to come in only to discover I wasn't lying about the complex changing the locks. He called and texted a few times, and when I wouldn't answer the door, he left with his clothes, books, and other belongings.

Everything went quiet. My apartment was much emptier than it had been that morning, and my body was so hyped up on adrenaline that I coasted through the night. I don't remember much of it, but I do know that part of me hoped that would be the end of it.

***

The next four days were paralyzing. There was no end to the calls, texts, letters, and roses that Chase left on my doorstep every day. He finally admitted that he didn't file a police report because he didn't think the police would help that much and he wanted to handle the break-in so I wouldn't have to. He apologized a million times and was certain that we could work through it.

Meanwhile, I was spending a lot of time at my dad's house so I had company and someone to talk to. It was the weekend of New Year's Eve. To celebrate the New Year and keep me company, my dad and his girlfriend made a delicious dinner and watched a cheesy movie with me. I was home and in bed by 10:30 p.m., wondering if I was really going to spend every night by myself again. Is this how I would start my year?

Thankfully, no one was telling me what I should do because I didn't think I could handle anyone's advice or criticism. I was sad, confused, lost, and not sure who I could talk to or what my next steps would be. How could I call the police on the person I had planned on spending forever with? At the same time, I knew I couldn't keep living in fear of him showing up every day with flowers, trying to talk to me.

Finally, on Tuesday, January 3, my dad reminded me of a dear friend who was the lead practitioner at our church. The practitioners at Mile Hi are different from a typical counselor or therapist. "Practitioner" means someone who practices, and these bright souls not only continuously practice holding space and praying for all of us, but they help us see our highest and best selves. Instead of giving us advice, they guide us to find the answers and the Divine Spirit, which is already our truth—we just get so caught up in the human world that we forget sometimes. Instead of counselors, I think of them as spiritual coaches.

I called the lead practitioner and asked for a recommendation of someone to talk to about what was going on. She suggested I call Lyla. I had already met with Lyla several years earlier for guidance with my previous boyfriend, and I thanked my friend for the perfect reminder.

Lyla is one of my angels on this earth. She held our first session that evening over Zoom. After an hour of her listening and holding space for me, I realized I needed to call the police. Only some people will ever understand the inability to report the love of my life, even after what he did. But the fear I was living in was worse, and I needed it to end.

The police officer came over and got the entire story on paper. It was surprising to see the shock on his face. I had thought they dealt with this kind of thing more often. He told me he would turn it over to a detective first thing in the morning and someone would give me a call. I guess part of me felt relieved, but to be honest, a lot of this is still a blur, and only certain details stand out.

Too impatient to wait, I called the detective the next morning to see if he had any updates. The detective started by asking me a bunch of questions, most of which I remember.

"Miss Dalby, how long were you and Chase together?"

"Three years."

"And did he know where the gold bar was?"

"Yes."

"Did he have permission to access the safe and the gold bar?" I could tell he was asking for legal purposes because he already knew the answer.

"No. He used to have a key to my safe, but I took that back from him." I'd given Chase a key for a while to keep his things in the safe, but I'd taken it back over a year prior, after one of our big arguments.

"Do you have any pictures of the bar?"

"No, it was a gift, and I never thought to take pictures of it."

"Okay, when was the last time you remember seeing the gold bar?"

The hair on the back of my neck stood on end. "Ummm, honestly, I don't know. I put it in the safe a year ago, then maybe saw it in the spring or summer when I was cleaning things out." At this point, I was a little embarrassed. It felt silly that I hadn't checked on a piece of gold worth ten thousand dollars more often.

"Well, I have some news that might come as a shock to you. We can run reports of all sales to all of the pawn shops in the Denver metro area. Whenever you sell something to a pawn shop, you have to show your ID and sign for it. The report shows that Chase sold the gold bar to a pawn shop in Westminster back on June 16, 2022."

That was six months ago. The silence seemed to last for minutes.

"Wait. What? Are you serious?"

"Yes." The detective sounded very hesitant, like he was waiting for my reaction.

"Why would he stage a break-in now if he sold it back in June?" I was half dazed and half numb.

"Honestly, we may never find that answer."

The rest of the conversation focused on the logistics of what would happen next. The detective was sure that the pawn shop had long since melted down the gold bar, but if he could get Chase to admit that he did it, I could get restitution in the amount that he sold it for. He would call Chase later that afternoon to get a statement from him and let me know when he had updates.

"Do you feel safe in your apartment, Miss Dalby?" he asked.

"Yes, I don't think Chase would do anything." I really was sure of that at the time.

"Okay, call 911 immediately if he decides to show up at your house. I will make sure he knows you want no contact from him."

I hung up and sat at the park for quite some time, staring at the water and wondering if I would ever feel like I was living my life again.

A lot happened over the next two days. Chase continued to leave flowers and letters on my doorstep, explaining how sorry he was and how he would change his habits going forward. Meanwhile, the detective couldn't get in touch with him, so I felt like I was at a standstill. I couldn't keep coming back to my apartment, scared that Chase might be waiting for me. It was the last thing I wanted to do, but I decided to file a protection order.

I called the courts on Thursday afternoon, and they explained that I could only file a protection order at certain times. The next time would be Monday morning between 7 a.m. and 9 a.m. The little amount of sleep I was getting would only get worse by then, so I took my cat and some of my belongings and moved in with my brother for the weekend. Thank God for siblings who take care of us.

The Friday I moved in with my brother, I got a call from the detective.

"Hi, Miss Dalby. Have you heard from Chase today?"

"No, I blocked his phone number." This was something I was actually really proud of.

"Well, I received a message from him just now admitting to the whole thing—he said that he was in financial trouble over the summer, so he sold the gold bar to buy himself some time, with the intention of replacing it. He hadn't replaced it yet last month and knew that you would notice it was missing based on some of the gifts you received for Christmas, so he staged the break-in to make it look like someone else had done it. He also said he wanted to admit all of this to you before he came in to talk to me, so could you have your brother or someone unblock his phone number to get this confession, and I can add it to the case notes?"

Somehow, the detective's explanation didn't surprise me. It was like he was confirming what I already knew.

And yet, it made it ten times worse. On the verge of tears, I told him that I could do that and I would send him the confession once I got it. I'll never forget how he ended the conversation.

"I'm really sorry about the gold bar, but at least you'll get restitution."

"I could care less about the money. I just lost my person," I said, unable to hold back the tears anymore.

"I'm so sorry." And he hung up.

Chapter 6

The Beginning

The night after I spoke with the detective, I unblocked Chase's number and sent him a text saying I knew he had something to tell me. He replied with the same information that he had sent the detective, and all I could do was read it over and over and over. I was at peace and, at the same time, completely heartbroken. I ended the conversation by telling Chase I would block his number again and that I would always love him—something that still rings true.

Monday morning, I took his confession text along with photos of all the letters he had left me to the courthouse. My dear friend Jackie drove with me and sat for two and a half hours, holding my hand the entire time. I filled out the paperwork and stood in front of a judge to explain why I felt I needed a protection order—something I wouldn't wish on my worst enemy. No matter how kind the judge was, no one should ever have to stand in front of one and explain why the person they love most should be kept away. He granted a temporary order, which I took to the sheriff's department to have served to Chase.

I learned that when you file a protection order, at least in the state of Colorado, it is temporary for fourteen days. After that time, both parties must go back to court to determine one of three outcomes:

1. Both parties decide to drop the order completely.
2. The person who filed the order decides they would like it to become permanent. At that time, both parties would sit through a trial explaining and defending their side of the story as to why it should or should not become permanent.
3. Both parties agree to extend the temporary order for a specific amount of time, up to a year, after which they can decide to drop the order completely or go back to trial to make it permanent.

I spent all fourteen days debating what to do. The obvious answer was to make the order permanent so I didn't have to deal with this again. However, the thought of standing in court and trying to prove my case while having to listen to Chase debate his side of the story, if that was what he would do, was unbearable. The thought of seeing him again was already too much, let alone going through a hearing. The anticipation was agony.

As I mentioned earlier, there are angels in this world who come into our lives for a reason, and another such angel who crossed my path was from an organization called Family Tree. They help victims of domestic abuse and violence with housing, finances, protection, legal matters, and much more. When I called to explain my predicament, a woman called me back and answered all my questions. She talked me through every scenario and possible outcome and listened without judgment. I was so grateful to have her in my corner, and she even offered to sit in court with me as moral support on the day of the hearing.

The fourteen days passed, and I still didn't know what decision to make when the judge asked what I wanted to do. This was one I couldn't plan or control without experiencing debilitating anxiety, so I decided to let go and trust. I meditated and prayed for an hour before leaving my house just for the strength to show up calm enough to sit through the process. It was all I could do to get in the car and drive to the courthouse. Chase's car was already there when I arrived twenty minutes early.

I was relieved to have the Family Tree representative with me, but she made it very clear that she would not be able to help once Chase and I stood in front of the judge. She answered my last-minute questions before we walked in, then took a seat next to me to hold space while we waited. Chase sat on the opposite side of the courtroom.

We were one of six protection order cases that afternoon,

and after forty minutes of listening to the other cases, we were the last ones called to the bench. As I sat down, I made sure to read the top of my notebook, which said in big letters, "BREATHE."

The judge read through his mandatory statements and confirmed that we both understood. Then he turned to me and asked how I would like to proceed with the case. I told him that I would like to extend the temporary order for the full year. This would give me time to heal and process before I had to decide my next steps, and I wouldn't have to sit through a hearing that day. The judge turned to Chase and asked if he agreed with that outcome.

Chase responded, "Anything she wants, I will agree to."

It took a total of six minutes, during which we were sent back to our seats to wait for the paperwork to print. The judge explained that I would leave the courtroom first, then Chase would need to wait three to five minutes after I left to avoid any confrontation.

Bewildered as to what had just happened, I breathed a sigh of relief when I got to my car. It felt like this was a huge step in my healing process. Maybe I could finally start moving forward. I texted my friends and family, and they all shared how happy they were for me to have gotten through the last two weeks and the court case. For a split second, it felt like it was over. That feeling didn't last long, though.

The next morning, I woke with more emotions than I had ever felt at one time. I was relieved to know I was safe in my space and I didn't have to go back to court, exhausted after coming down from all the adrenaline I had built up the day before, confused as to what would happen next in the legal process regarding the theft, but most of all, I felt completely devastated. Devastated to wake up and realize that at that moment, I was by myself. Chase would not be coming back. I wouldn't hear from him again, and my plan for our life together had come to a screeching halt then disappeared with no closure. I had lost my person, my friend, and the love that I had planned on spending my future with.

What do you do when your whole world changes in the blink of an eye? How was I supposed to rebuild my life? How would I ever go back out in public? What would I tell people when they asked what happened? Was I just supposed to pick back up where I left off and try to "move on"?

I had no more paperwork to prepare, no more phone calls with the police or houses to move from—just me and my thoughts as I tried to put the pieces back together. I spent most of that day sitting on my couch, attempting to drown out the noise in my head and ignore the question I couldn't let go of. What's next?

It was the beginning of an entirely new life.

Section 2
Healing Waves

I've seen a diagram on social media before that shows two different versions of success. The first one is "What we think success should look like," and it's a straight line upwards. The second is "What success actually looks like," and it's a bundle of squiggly lines that move in circles and sideways and up and down, eventually finding its way forward.

This feels like an accurate representation of healing. We so deeply wish it would be a straight and easy line, and sometimes, it is, but many times, it moves in directions that we can't predict, and we just have to do our best and hold on through the ups and downs.

I once told Lyla that I felt like the pinball in this process, being tossed around, surrounded by loud noises and chaos. Other days, I felt like I was on a roller coaster, screaming for dear life. Lyla held the space for me, as she always does, then kindly redirected my ideas.

"Instead of a roller coaster, what if they are waves? And you're just surfing the waves as they come and go?"

I liked that picture a lot better than a loud pinball machine or a screaming roller coaster. So I started to surf the waves of healing—the joy, the grief, the love, and the crashes.

Chapter 7

Grief

No one word can describe the next four months of my life. January through April was tumultuous, empty, progressive, heartbreaking, groundbreaking, eye-opening, and everything in between. The range of feelings I experienced was endless, all of which could be summed up in the broad category of "numb." Put simply, I was grieving—over and over and over again.

Two weeks into January, I was taking a workout class at the gym where I coached. It had been an emotional morning, and I was using the workout to relieve stress, like I had done a thousand times before. Five minutes into the workout, with a barbell on my shoulders, I came up out of a squat and immediately felt my back give out. Being a fitness professional and not wanting to admit a trainer's worst nightmare, I slowly finished the workout and decided I would sleep it off and feel better the next day.

The following morning brought pain that had me hunched over and barely able to walk down the stairs to my car. I went to a massage therapist, who relieved a small amount of the discomfort, but that specific back injury had me out of commission and on the couch for almost a week. It would be another four months before I could start a slow and very light workout routine again. Not only was fitness my career, but it was my passion and part of who I was. Healing emotionally without it would feel impossible at times.

A month later, I came home from a haircut and started to feel extremely ill. To spare you the details, my body had not purged like that since I was a small kid. I got so sick that I ended up calling 911 and spending two nights (one of those days being Valentine's Day) in the ICU with norovirus. In case you're unfamiliar, like I was, norovirus is a nasty virus that causes vomiting and diarrhea; however, it doesn't usually send people to the hospital. That season, it was really bad, and the nurse told me six other people in their mid-thirties were in the ICU with it at the same time. My aunt would later comment that my body had purged itself of more than just the virus, and I think she was right.

As I lay in the hospital bed the second night, it was the first time in my life that I began to question if I still wanted to exist on this earth. The last six weeks had been the most painful I had ever been through, and it just kept coming. My losses and grief were monumental, and nothing was a quick fix. Healing your gut after norovirus is no easy task, and it just added to the list of ways that I felt my life wasn't working. If my life had a point, I couldn't see it. That both scared me and gave me some peace of mind. If I didn't want to exist, I wouldn't have to try, but I'd never had those feelings before, and I had no idea what to do with them. What do you do when you don't want to be here anymore?

I am still here today for many reasons, one of which is my spiritual community. After struggling through everything I had experienced, I once asked a mentor of mine how anyone survives this life without such a community, and her response was that's why she believes there is so much anxiety, depression, and illness in our society—simply put, we can't do this alone, and we can't do this without something greater to believe in.

My spiritual community, Mile Hi Church, is one of the greatest gifts my dad ever gave me, and he gave me many. He bribed me to go to church on Sunday mornings as a kid by promising me chocolate-glazed doughnuts afterward, and it worked. I am so grateful to say that this community has gotten me through some of the best and worst times of my life. It's through this community that I met Lyla, who has now been my spiritual coach for over a year. It's through this community that I attended a workshop about grief in February of 2023 that gave me a reason to start over.

Dr. Patty led this workshop one Sunday after church. The room was full of people grieving in many different ways—over death, finances, fear of the world's fate, rifts in families, breakups, divorces, illness, etc. Each one of us showed up for a different reason, and yet, I felt as though we were all looking for the same thing—a safe space to express our grief and have someone bring us a little bit of hope for what came next. Dr. Patty did just that. She spoke many truths that day, two of which have stuck with me.

First, grief is not linear or time specific. As much as our logical brains want to conceptualize grief, we cannot put a timeline to how or when our feelings will change and move. One step doesn't come after another, because we each experience grief differently. We may have experienced a loss twenty years ago, and when a song comes on the radio, it sets us right back to where we were when the loss first happened. Allowing ourselves to move through grief at whatever time it appears is part of healing.

Second, we cannot work through our grief unless we allow ourselves to fully feel our emotions. I learned much more about this in the coming months, but our bodies become sick and anxious when we shove away our emotions and "move on" with life, which is what most of us have been trained to do. Most of us have never learned a safe way to express how we feel. We are told that it's weak to show these emotions to others. So we put on a smile and keep walking through life as usual.

Society makes both of these truths difficult to work through because, as a whole, we are uncomfortable with grief. It's not easy to be with someone experiencing deep pain that we have not known in the same way, and we want people to move through it so we don't have to stay uncomfortable with them for very long. Each one of us has what we feel, consciously or subconsciously, is an acceptable time for someone to grieve a certain loss. Once that time expires, we tend to check out or rush the person through their process, probably without knowing that we are doing it. Realizing this truth and knowing that I could feel my grief anyway gave me a slightly stronger base to move forward on.

Not only did hearing these things put me a little more at ease, but seeing the roomful of people who felt as empty as I did gave me a little bit of comfort. I wasn't alone in my grief, though I was the only one who had gone through exactly what I had. We were all hurting together, and there were people who could walk alongside me in different ways to help me through the mud. I just had to be vulnerable enough to share my emotions so I could find those people.

Chapter 8

My Team of Angels

Loneliness can be a strange thing. After losing Chase, I felt lonelier than I ever had before. Not only did my apartment feel empty and unsafe, but no one knew exactly what I was going through or how to help. I am very blessed to have incredible family and friends who are always there for me, and yet, no matter how lonely I felt, I didn't want to be around them. I was so stuck in my grief that I had no desire to go out in public, and I certainly didn't want to tell the story over and over again. I couldn't go to baby showers or engagement parties because they reminded me of the future I had lost. It took every ounce of me to spend time with our mutual friends because it reminded me of all the times we'd spent together. And hearing everyone's opinions about how terrible Chase had been just rubbed salt in the wound, even if they were trying to help. Being at home with my thoughts was agony, and so was being around anyone else.

For me, one of the hardest parts about being in public while grieving was that no one knew what to say, and most people didn't say the right thing. Their hearts were all in the right place, and to be fair, what do you say to someone whose partner of three years stole ten thousand dollars from them? I truly believe that as humans, our nature is to want to help and try to comfort—we just aren't taught how to do that. "I'm sorry" and "What an asshole" didn't really feel grounding for me.

We can't go through this life alone, though, and during certain times, some people stand out who I think are meant to be our support squad. Lyla, for example, listened to me tell the same stories over and over again. She sat there without judgment and showed me that having a safe space to talk things out made a world of difference for me. To this day, she still encourages me to embrace exactly where I am with my feelings. She has also taught me the value of writing—when we have something in our brains that won't stop rolling, getting it on paper can be an amazing outlet if we have no other way to express our deepest thoughts.

I also had friends who held space for me to do nothing other than be together. I remember one evening when I felt a panic attack coming on and called a dear friend of mine. She left the dinner she was at so I could meet her at her house and feel safe. Jackie, the one who had taken me to the courthouse, and her husband cooked me dinner on numerous occasions and let me sit with them on their couch without needing to say anything. One night, my dad took me out to dinner, not having a clue what to say, but he sat across the table from me just so I knew he was there. If this experience has taught me anything, it's that most of the time, the best support we can give someone is to simply be present. Not try to fix anything or say anything, just sit there and hold space.

My acupuncturist, Ashlie—who is more of a spiritual coach than I think she realizes—let me cry and yell for twenty minutes at the beginning of our sessions every time I saw her. Because of her open heart, we brought together a group of spiritual sisters who now form a meditation group where I've received support on many levels. And I met a new physical therapist, Beth Anne, who taught me what it means to heal our nervous systems after we experience trauma. It was because of her that I rearranged my entire bedroom and bought a night-light so I could feel safe enough to get more than three or four hours of sleep a night.

I share all these stories because being vulnerable enough to ask for help can be hard. Many of us are taught that asking for help is weak. We are afraid that people will judge us if we share our true feelings. "Rub some dirt on it" still carries weight in our society, and some believe that you should pick yourself up by your bootstraps and get on with life because it makes you stronger. These are valid fears, and we may lose some people in our lives who aren't comfortable if we show up authentically.

However, I might not be here without the friends and family who show up for me every single day. Without their presence, I definitely would not be healing the way I am. My relationships transformed during this time because I started to do the brutally uncomfortable and hard work of asking for what I needed and showing up as I really felt—even if that meant crying on someone's couch for two hours.

On many occasions in the coming year, I was challenged to face this head-on, and I'm still working on it today. I grew relationships into clarity and honesty, I shared some very difficult conversations with loved ones, and I also lost some long-term friendships, which was very painful. The shell I had built my whole life started to break open enough that I had no capacity to show up as anything other than what I was. This authenticity and growth called in a team of angels that I hope we are all brave enough to look for in our lifetimes.

Chapter 9

Controlling the Uncontrollable

While I worked to calm my emotions, connect with my support system, and heal my physical body, a legal storm brewed behind the scenes. To share all the details would take an entire book in itself. Never before had I learned so much about our legal system, and to be frank, I didn't care to learn so much. But when someone commits a felony against you, you must partake in a certain process.

There was a dichotomy in the things I could ask for and the things I couldn't, some of which changed each time I spoke with a representative from the city. The first person who got in contact with me was a woman from the victim's advocate department. Their job is to support individuals who have been affected by any sort of crime by helping with financial and security resources. For example, she told me I could get reimbursed for my security system and counseling if my spiritual coach qualified. She also told me they would send housing resources if I didn't feel safe in my home. I had no idea these were options for people in this kind of situation, and I felt somewhat relieved to have their support.

The next person I interacted with for a few weeks was the detective. After he received Chase's confession, he called me and asked how I wanted to proceed. To be honest, I was shocked that I had a choice in the matter. I just assumed these things followed a standard protocol. He asked if I wanted them to arrest Chase on the spot and put a bail on his release or if I wanted them to deliver a summons to him to appear in court and set a date for his hearing. I chose the latter.

It took at least a month for the court to set the first court date. Within that time, a victim's advocate from Family Tree contacted me and put me in touch with the attorney who would oversee the case on my behalf. During the weeks between the hearing notice and speaking with the attorney, I was asked to fill out legal statements, applications for reimbursement, restitution requests, and other documentation restating what had happened.

The attorney called me the night before the first hearing to ask how I wanted the outcome of the hearing to end. With no clue what my options were, I asked her to run through them with me and recommend a reasonable request from the defense attorney. Of course, this included restitution for what was stolen, among other things, like asking that Chase take a behavioral assessment and be required to take domestic violence classes as part of his probation. I agreed with her recommendations, and at the end of the phone call, she said they would keep me updated as the hearings progressed.

Up to this point, I felt overwhelmed, but at the same time, I felt like I had inserted my voice enough to have a say in what happened. Part of me saw a light at the end of the tunnel. It seemed as though the attorney would ask the judge for exactly what I requested, and Chase would go through a transformation as part of the correctional process. I had even spoken with Lyla about the option of going through group counseling with Chase once everything calmed down in the hopes that he might understand the repercussions of his actions. For me, loving someone not only means wanting the best for them but also the best for us, which I hoped might mean a friendship in the long run.

These hopes diminished over the coming months for several reasons. The first three hearings Chase had (thankfully, I did not need to attend) took less than thirty seconds and consisted of the judge and/or attorneys asking for a new hearing date. They kept extending the case for various reasons, some having to do with Chase, but most having to do with the logistics of how the legal system works and people being out of town.

Almost five months after the original incident, on May 22, 2023, the final hearing occurred. At that time, I had not received any logistical updates from the attorney. I had sent one email restating my wishes, but we had not spoken after that. Part of me assumed that she would have at least checked in before the hearing, as I would later find out that a lot had happened behind the scenes. However, I also learned that the victims in most felony cases don't have a say in the matter. I was only somewhat involved because it was deemed a domestic violence case.

I was able to watch the hearing online. Chase and his attorney were the last case to be called up to the podium. The judge matter-of-factly stated the charges that Chase was accused of, asked the attorneys what they wished to see happen, signed the document, and went about his day. The decision? Chase would pay me what was stolen in restitution, and he would be on probation for a year, which would be extended if necessary. Nothing else was mentioned about the other programs the attorney and I had originally spoken about. Five months of waiting, and it was over in a matter of minutes.

My initial reaction was utter defeat. After everything that I had suffered and been through since Christmas, it felt like he had received a slap on the wrist. He would go about his life, working and writing me checks every month, and I was left with the pieces I was still trying to put back together. I was the one who didn't feel safe in her apartment, who wasn't sleeping at night, whose physical body was still mending, who didn't feel comfortable around her friends.

It felt like my wishes had not been heard, that this was an everyday occurrence, and the legal system was not about to ensure that the decision they made brought peace to anyone else involved. It felt like rock bottom all over again.

The thing about rock bottom is that we have a choice. We can choose to stay there, stuck as victims, listening to how the rest of the world would write our story, or we can get angry enough to change the story. Anger is a powerful emotion, though we are taught that it's not appropriate to be angry. It's a turning point, an optional pivot point, if we choose to see it that way. Emotions are gifts that bring us messages, and anger sometimes shows up to say, "Hey, you're not being treated the way you want to be. What are you going to do about it?"

So I made a choice—clearly, the legal system wouldn't take care of me the way I felt it should have. Looking back from a more compassionate point of view, they truly are just humans like you and me, who are overloaded with more work than they have the capacity to handle every day. They do the best they can with what they have, and putting my happiness in their hands would be like asking a fisherman who nets hundreds of fish a day to pull out the one shiny rainbow trout in the bunch.

I decided not to give my power to someone else that way. The outcome hadn't turned out the way I'd wanted it to, and I couldn't change that. Suffering comes from trying to control the things we cannot, which is everything and everyone but ourselves. So, I allowed myself to feel my anger, I did the work with my spiritual coach, and I made the choice to keep moving forward with my life. Letting go is not easy, and I found support where I needed it. Continuing to heal my nervous system, setting boundaries where required, and focusing my time on my passions again were my next steps in moving forward.

Chapter 10

Authenticity to Empowerment

Dealing with the legal system taught me that there comes a point in the healing journey when it's time to start taking back our power. When we experience certain traumas, our legs are cut from underneath us. To stand again, we must look to outside sources to help us rebuild and feel stable. I was extremely fortunate to have the people and experiences I needed to help me regain myself. Not only did I partake in weekly spiritual coaching, but I healed through acupuncture, physical therapy, Reiki, podcasts/videos, writing, group sessions, and advice from loved ones. It had all gotten me to a point where I started to feel whole again, and for that, I am so grateful.

As I did this healing work, I began to feel uncomfortable with some of the outside voices and their advice.

Everything people told me was said out of love and protection, but some of it was not in alignment with my values. As I took more steps out of the fog, I could reconnect with my voice and authentically see what I wanted my healing and my life to look like. I became more aligned with my higher self, even when others did not agree with how that manifested.

I will be forever grateful to my aunt for pushing me into one such moment. She was in town, visiting for Easter weekend, and she and my gram and I went out to lunch. It was the first time I had seen my aunt in person since everything had happened, and the first fifteen minutes of the conversation felt like the forced casual talk I had gotten pretty good at faking when I was out in public or with loved ones.

Then she looked at me point-blank and said, "So, sweetheart, tell me what's going on with Chase. Whatever you want to share, if you want to."

Immediate dread hit my stomach like it always did when this topic came up. I reluctantly gave her the surface-level version of where we were in the legal process and what paperwork I was in the middle of, keeping it logistical and just about the facts.

To be honest, I don't remember what she said next, and I don't remember how the conversation changed, but for the first time in a while, I started to blurt what was really going on.

"Honestly, Aunt Leann, I don't want to be here. I don't see a purpose in life anymore. I'm not sleeping. I'm not eating, and I'm in a really dark place."

Without blinking, she looked at me and said, "Well, of course you are. And that's completely okay."

It was the first time I had been truly honest with anyone besides Lyla and the first time someone else had told me it was okay. She didn't try to fix it. She didn't tell me it would get better. She didn't freak out that I would do something rash. She just sat there and made it completely safe for me to say what I needed to say.

"It's really hard to be around people right now because I can't show up as my normal, cheerful self. I can't sit there and pretend like I'm okay when I'm not," I continued.

"So, why don't you let someone else take on that role for once? Why don't you let someone else lead the conversation for a bit? You might find you don't have to if someone else has the chance."

I'll never forget that lunch because it was one of the moments I started to pivot back into my power. Aunt Leann reminded me that, though it was messy and uncomfortable, I could still show up as my authentic self in the dark times. I didn't have to put on a mask for the people I loved because they would be there to love me still.

That night, the night before Easter, I went home and shaved my head. It wasn't about making a statement—it was about letting go of everyone else's perceptions of me and releasing the old energy I carried. I was ready to show up in any form that felt most comfortable, even when others would tell me I was crazy for doing it.

Chapter 11

Choices

I can count on one hand the number of people who know the next part of my story. I mentioned in the last chapter that as I started to step into my power again, I made choices not everyone agreed with. The last thing I needed was to hear all the opinions that would come with some of these choices, so I took care of myself by keeping certain things between me and Lyla. As a people pleaser, this was hard for me because I felt like I was keeping secrets. In hindsight, it was the best way for me to heal and give myself grace. Especially with the gravity of some of my decisions.

As part of my healing, I wrote regular letters to Chase, which I kept in an envelope. Writing truly can be therapeutic, and by putting my thoughts on paper, I could express my emotions and the thoughts that I couldn't in person. It was a way of getting them out of my head so I could focus on other things. When the time was right, I would burn the letters to help release the energy I had been holding onto.

After a few months of writing, I had collected eight or nine letters. They ranged from cussing at Chase for what he had done to letting him go, to thanking him for everything he had given me in our relationship, to asking him every question I couldn't, then back to rage. Every time I finished a letter, I felt a little more relieved, however, something still unsettled my soul.

The urge to talk to Chase wouldn't go away. It just kept getting stronger. Though I had been through breakups before, they had been completely different circumstances, and after a month or two, that urge usually died down. Not this time. The more time passed, the harder it was to keep the letters to myself.

I told one of my mentors about this, and she insisted that absolutely under no circumstances could I ever talk to Chase again because his energy would just pull me back in. She said that he needed to do his own work and I wouldn't be able to discern from his truth or lies if I started talking to him. However right or wrong she was, I felt judged by her words, which fueled my fire and made me want to talk to him more.

When I brought it up with Lyla, she asked me a few logistical questions about the protection order in place, asked about how I would handle certain outcomes, then told me, at the end of the day, it was my decision. (One of the reasons we get along so well is because she never tells me what to do—she simply asks questions to get me to think about my path.)

So, I called my contact at Family Tree and asked her what the legal implications would be if I were to reach out to Chase with the protection order in place. She told me that nothing would happen unless he responded and I decided to report it because I was the one who had initiated the protection order. I already knew that if I reached out to him, I would take accountability for reopening the line of communication. I couldn't take it back or blame him for responding.

Once I got off the phone, I weighed the answers my contact gave me with the conversation I'd had with Lyla. This was a really big decision. There were so many ways that it could go wrong and so many logical reasons why I should keep to myself. At the end of the day, however, I had already set my mind, and no one could say anything to change that. I couldn't ignore my soul anymore.

I collected the letters, put them in a box, took a deep breath, and mailed them to Chase.

Section 3
Talking with God

My spirituality doesn't believe in God as one person who is far away, looking down on us all and deciding what will happen in our lives. Instead, we believe that God is the one true energy from which all things are born and which exists in and as each living being. This energy that we call Spirit, Divine Love, God, Source, Life, etc. moves and expresses as all life and is, therefore, the guiding Light that we can all cocreate and communicate with.

I feel closest to God when I meditate or when I'm in nature, but in truth, I don't have to go anywhere or do anything to find it. Spirit is my Truest Self and the call of my heart, which is always talking to me and sending me signs and synchronicities. It can be scary to listen to this Spirit when it gives us an answer that we know others won't understand, but it's also the most authentic version of our lives when we choose to align with it. It's always supporting our highest and best.

Chapter 12

It's the Heart That Ruffles Feathers

I've spent a lot of my life dancing between two lifestyles. The first—people pleasing because it's the "right" thing to do, even if I'm ignoring my boundaries to do so. The second—ruffling feathers just to prove a point because I really don't like it when people put me in a box and tell me how I should live my life.

The decision to talk to Chase again was a third and brand-new category for me—I guess I would call it heart following. I didn't tell anyone I was talking to him at first, so I had no motivation to people please or ruffle feathers. I was simply following what my heart told me to do. Though I'm one hundred percent certain that it would have ruffled everyone's feathers if I had told my friends and family that we were talking again.

At first, after he received the letters, I reached out to him on social media. That turned into texting, and eventually, we met up to walk and talk. The conversations were deep, hurtful, pointless, and meaningful all at the same time. We talked about life, the court process, what had happened between us, and everything in between. It was surreal and yet comforting. The words that had sat on my heart for four months were finally free.

By the time Chase and I started hanging out regularly again, both my mom and Lyla knew that we were in what I would call a friendship. Lyla would simply ask questions to make me think, and my mom, the amazing soul that she is, just listened. She knows me well enough that I think she understood nothing she said would change my course of action and she would rather be there to listen than speak her mind and push me away. What a blessing it was to have her nonjudgmental support. (Or at least she didn't judge me out loud—though I'm sure she had her opinions.)

To be completely honest, a small part of me wondered if Chase and I would get back together. Logistically, I knew it was impossible for a million and one reasons, and I couldn't see how I could ever be with someone who my family and friends would never have a relationship with again. But as cliché as it sounds, love does strange things to the heart. And I still loved him despite the immense hurt he had caused.

I'll tell you the rest of the story in the following chapters, but if you're like my mom, who reads the last chapter of a book to know the conclusion, Chase and I did not end up together. We went through some very high highs and some extremely low lows from May through October. I'll share with you some of what I experienced, but at the end of the day, I am so glad that I made the decision to talk to him again. It confirmed the choice I needed to make multiple times, and I am fortunate to have had the opportunity to see it.

I want to make one point here about the power of the heart and the things that we will never understand about each other. I used to believe that I knew exactly what was best for the people I loved because I cared about them and wanted to protect them. It's hard to watch someone make choices for their life that we disagree with because it may hurt them in the long run. And if I hadn't gone through this experience, I might still believe that.

However, now I understand that we will never know exactly what someone is going through and where their heart is taking them. Even if everyone on the outside thinks they see the right path, we will never truly feel what someone endures, and we can't make that decision for them. The heart is a strong muscle, and it will pull us in ways that no one else might understand.

I believe this is part of the human experience—listening to our hearts even when they may lead us down a difficult path. It is our responsibility, and ours alone, to make the choices in life that allow us to experience it fully. That includes the beautiful decisions as well as the unpopular ones.

Chapter 13

Hiking Therapy

Summer was my time to process everything that had happened since Christmas. Chase and I were talking off and on—we would work on things then get in an argument and stop talking for weeks at a time. I was figuring out what my next path in life was as far as my career, and my physical healing was taking more time than my impatient self would allow.

One of the ways I worked through everything was hiking. I had enjoyed doing it since college, but this summer was different. It was no longer about how fast I could hike to the top or how many fourteeners I could conquer. This summer was about clearing my head and working through my thoughts that kept spiraling.

Almost every Friday, I tried a new trail, and every Friday, I had a new experience. The amount of truth that comes through the mind when you pull away other thoughts and distractions is magic. During one of these hikes I went on with Chase, I asked him what he thought our purpose was on Earth. With so much hurt and pain and destruction, why live? Why should anyone have kids to keep moving on in this mess of a world? His response was simple—"Maybe that is our purpose. To find the beauty in all the chaos and live in that space because that beauty is needed." That gave me a strange peace to move forward.

A couple of weeks later, I was hiking in the rain, which turned to thunder and lightning. No, it's not safe to hike during a thunderstorm, but once you're halfway through a trail, the best way back to safety is to keep going.

I remember taking what I thought was the last big switchback only to come to another steep hill. I sighed in exhaustion and started screaming at the thunder and lightning as I climbed.

"Fine! Come and get me, God! What's the point of living? If I'm going to die, I might as well do it on a mountain in a thunderstorm! My life is complete, and I don't care anymore! I dare you to strike me down! Let's go!"

I screamed and cried and screamed some more. I was so angry, so full of frustration for what I felt like the world had dealt me the last seven months. And I didn't care if I lived or died in that moment. It felt as though the universe was challenging me to keep going to the top of that hill, to risk it all, so I did. I climbed through the thunderstorm, yelling until I had no more words to scream.

It's exhilarating to let go that much, to truly surrender to whatever life delivers. I'm working on living in that type of surrender for the rest of my life—to be free enough to know that I don't have to resist or force my future. I just have to let go and be willing to, sometimes, climb in a thunderstorm. Much easier said than done.

There were plenty of hikes after that one, where I didn't risk my life, and I continued to work through my soul-stirring questions about our existence on this planet. I'm not sure if I came out of it all with more or less questions about why we are here and what our souls are supposed to be doing in this lifetime, but I did feel more supported and connected after each one.

Serendipitously, that same summer, during a Sunday service at church, one of the ministers said, "Sometimes, we wonder if we are done here on this earth. Well, let me tell you. If you're still here, you still have work to do."

I guess I wasn't supposed to die on the mountain that day.

Chapter 14

Sometimes Standing Alone Is the Best Place to Stand

A feeling that never really left me was loneliness. A lot of my friends get busy during the summertime, and some of my relationships had changed because, well, I had changed. The connections I was forming were different from what they had been in the past. On top of that, I had spent the previous summer traveling and camping with Chase, so this summer felt like a huge hole in my life.

I'm a fixer, like many people, and when I feel uncomfortable with something, I try to fix it. So I got on Meetup and joined a bunch of groups that interested me. It was all great and dandy until it came time to actually attend one of the meetings. That felt sticky and forced and not authentic to myself. It didn't seem genuine to attend one of these gatherings just to avoid loneliness.

When I brought it up with Lyla, of course, she had the perfect thing to say.

"Well, why do you feel like you need to go meet new people?" she asked.

"Part of me feels lonely. And the other part feels like I should be doing more things with more people. I don't want to be an outcast who's home alone all the time."

"I wonder if that's a negative self-judgment."

Lyla holds the highest and best space for self-forgiveness. She has taught me so much about the negative ways in which I judge myself and how to forgive myself for those judgments. In this case, it would be something like "I forgive myself for judging myself as lazy if I don't go out and meet new people." Having that self-compassion for our human experience can be such a transformation in allowing ourselves to let go of the unrealistic standards we may hold ourselves to. At the end of the day, we really are just humans trying to do our best.

By the end of the session, I realized I needed to allow myself to feel lonely—not fix it, not try to change it, just feel it. And everything that came with it—sadness, anger, fear, etc.

"Once you come to a place where you accept where you are and how you feel, I don't think you'll have to force new friendships or relationships. Your energy will attract the right people because you are in the right space." Another one of Lyla's soul-healing lessons.

So, with that feeling, I decided to take a camping trip on my own. I drove to Ouray, Colorado, and camped for three nights at one of the hot springs on the edge of town. Ouray is a small, spiritual city on the western side of Colorado that I had visited before. I feel very connected there, and I knew it was a safe space for me. It was the first trip I'd taken on my own in three years, and I was nervous to be alone.

The hot springs where I camped used to be owned by the Indigenous people who first settled there, and its natural water source has a high lithium content, which is super relaxing for the mind and body. It's a magical place that gets busy with locals and tourists during the day. At night, however, the pools are closed to anyone who isn't camping or staying on the property. Nine p.m. came, and everyone cleared out except me. For almost twenty minutes, I was alone in the healing waters, floating on my back, and staring up at the stars while it started to rain. It reminded me that I could do this, I could live this life even if I was scared to start again.

The next day, I went for a hike that encompasses the perimeter of the town. The view of the scenery and the city is incredible. I came across waterfalls, wildflowers, open fields, high peaks, and a gnarly climb right when I thought I should be heading back into town. I had a long conversation with God during that hike, feeling both happy and frustrated. But at the end of the day, I did it. I drove six hours by myself to camp and hike and reconnect with nature (the most healing of modalities, in my opinion), when two months earlier, I didn't think I would ever feel comfortable in this physical world again. One baby step at a time, with a lot of self-compassion, I was healing.

Two weeks after I returned home from that trip, I started a twelve-week business course with Jon Hillstead. Talk about attracting the right people into my life. If you don't know Jon, he is an incredibly bright soul who creates the space for others to live their authentic lives. I found him on Instagram, and the course that I signed up for was called Slay Your Way to 100k. I was ready to start taking my spiritual coaching to the next level and create my dream business.

The lessons I took away from those twelve weeks could be a book all by itself. I released the limiting beliefs I had been holding onto. I created a plan to publish this very book and start my speaking career. I solidified the vision of how I wanted to show up in the world, and I came into the fierceness of my power and creativity. What a blessing that course and that group of individuals were for me.

Out of everything I got from the experience, I still think about one lesson and live by it to this day. We discussed our various businesses and how we had all coached in the past, and I brought up a meditation class that I taught. After searching for the right venue, I had found a place with kind people, a good location, and the perfect space to teach meditation. The downfall was that I only had two or three people show up each time. However, I was so grateful to each of them for showing up, and honestly, they taught me just as much as I taught them. It was a good situation at the time.

When I brought that up in our group sharing, Jon said very simply, "Sometimes, you have to let go of good to go for great. Many of us hold on to situations or things because they are easy and good and comfortable. But what if letting go of that ease and comfort opens the space for something even greater to flood in?"

Mind blown.

That one phrase not only changed how I thought about my business, but it started to change my viewpoint on the friendship I held onto with Chase. It was comfortable and easy, and I didn't want to lose him. We fought just as much as we didn't, but it seemed good to me because I didn't have to go through the pain of losing him again, and I connected with him.

However, maybe it was time to let go of whatever good we had so I could create space for something greater.

Chapter 15

The Path Always Changes

I was getting back to living in my own skin. Hiking had become easier on my body. I could take workout classes. Jon's course was helping me move forward with what I wanted to do in life, and I felt my independence steering me away from Chase. I had even adopted a new kitten named Charlie, who brought a lot of lessons and, at the same time, a lot of laughter to my life. I was creating my new normal and my new way of being in the world.

That path changed on August 3. I came home that evening to an odd voicemail from my dad. He didn't sound like himself. All he said was that he wanted me to call him back. When I did, he explained to me that his doctor had found a mass on his pancreas. My dad had been experiencing some stomach issues for a few months, which had led to an MRI, where they'd found this mass.

The entire phone call was somewhat calm for both of

us. He went on to tell me that the next step was a biopsy to see if the mass was cancerous or not. That would take place on the fourteenth. If the tumor came back as benign, they would discuss whether it needed to be removed and, if so, how. If it came back as cancer, my dad would go through four weeks of chemotherapy and radiation to try shrinking the tumor, have surgery to remove as much of the tumor as they could, and then another six plus weeks of chemotherapy. It sounded pretty cut-and-dry when he explained it all.

To be honest, when I hung up the phone, I think my shock and naivety about the situation kept me calmer than expected. Of course it couldn't be cancer. This was my dad we were talking about. My family always gets through the obstacles we face in life, and this would be no different. They would find that the tumor was benign, remove it so my dad would feel better, and life would go on.

It took about a day for the reality to hit me. What if it was cancer? Ten-plus weeks of chemotherapy was no joke. Not to mention some of the people I was closest to who I shared this with brought up the fact that the survival rate of pancreatic cancer is only three to twelve percent. My family was worried, and now I was too.

I tried to pray about it, meditate on it, and hike it out, but this one was too big for me. There are some things in life that we just can't carry on our own. So I emailed one of the sacred souls from Mile Hi and asked him to hold space for our family and for my dad. It was too much weight for me to carry. I needed someone else to hold the space so I could release some of the thoughts running through my mind. He lovingly agreed.

Two weeks passed in agony for us all, and I got the phone call from Dad on August 16.

It was cancer.

Chapter 16

The Meaning of a Life

I won't share most of the details of my dad's journey with cancer, because that's not who he was. He wasn't his battle with cancer. He wasn't the cancer itself, and he wasn't the body that went through the journey. That was all just a small part of his story. I want him to be remembered for his soul, his big heart, his adventurous spirit, his bright smile, his amazing hugs, his annoying skill of always beating me at cards, his love of travel, his love of food, his love of his family, and most of all, his love for my brother and me.

I will share these things:

He was so strong the entire journey. He shared his heart with us.

He did absolutely everything in his power to beat it.

He still showed up for his family every single day.

He was stubborn just as he always had been.

He was able to have one last Sunday family dinner with all of us.

He and I were able to share laughs and memories in his final days.

He got to listen to Michael Franti one more time.

He and my mom got to say "I love you" one last time after twenty-four years of being divorced.

He was surrounded by all the love that he had shared until his last breath.

My dad passed away on October 7, 2023. He will always be one of my biggest cheerleaders, one of my greatest friends, and the most amazing dad I ever could have asked for.

I'll never let the world forget him.

Section 4
A
Legend

Chapter 17

Dad's Story

The following is the speech that I gave during my dad's celebration of life. More than two hundred people showed up to honor my dad that day. For the many people who didn't know him, this will give you a small glimpse of the incredible man that he was and part of his story. There is so much more to tell, and I know that will come with time. I'll continue to share his story as long as I live.

It should be acknowledged that there is an error in this speech when I bring up sporting events. Yes, I read it to everyone just as it's written, and yes, I realized after the fact that I had made it. But as my brother so lovingly said, "Cole, it was so authentically you. And it was just the right amount of humor that we all needed at the right time. It was perfect."

If you knew my dad, you're one of the lucky ones.

My dad lived with passion. I like to think he's where my passion for life came from. He never did anything halfway. He traveled where and when he wanted to, he ate at all the good restaurants and street fairs, he took me and Ty on wild adventures (even if we thought he was crazy), and he connected with people in the deepest way he knew how to. In April of 2022, he and I were blessed to go on a European cruise together, and I watched him smile big each time we got to taste or experience something new. His passion for the world and for life was contagious.

My dad was a sports fanatic. Golf and basketball were the two sports he loved the most, but he'd talk any kind of sport with Ty for hours. Sundays were for watching golf and football. Basketball was on anytime he could find a game. During the last year of his life, he and Ty had the opportunity to see the Avalanche play in the World Cup Series, and the Nuggets play in the Championship Series. They also got to attend a Duke–North Carolina basketball game, which was one of my dad's top bucket list items.

My dad was a friend. His friends from work, Juice Plus+, Up with People, sports, and school live around the world, and he had an impact on every one of them up until he made his transition. During the last weeks of his life, I received letter upon letter with nothing but love for my dad—how he gave the best hugs ever, how he supported people in their toughest times, how he was always friendly and smiling, and how he made people feel important. Even people who barely knew my dad had nothing but amazing things to say about him.

My dad was a coach—a basketball coach, to be specific, but also a life coach in his own way. Not only did he coach both me and Tyler's basketball teams, but he coached teams before and after us. He was the most passionate coach on the court (which sometimes got him into trouble), and he took care of every single player on his team. I remember him coming home to tell us about the life lessons he was teaching, not just the basketball drills. One of the letters he received in his last days was from a teammate of Tyler's, saying how not only did Dad coach him in basketball, but he taught him how to be a better person and hopefully an amazing dad one day. So many loved ones still call Dad "Coach' and will tell you that he impacted their lives on and off the court.

My dad was a son, a brother, and an uncle. He loved his family fiercely, and he would show up for every single one of us when we needed him to. He had his rough moments with his family, and he grew through them to show up the best way he knew how to. Aunt Leann's home is filled with cat figurines of every kind because that's what Dad would get her when he traveled. Sunday nights were always for family dinner at my grandparents' house, and my dad showed up to almost every single one. Even though he didn't always know how to express his emotions, he showed up the best he knew how to. Like a friend and former teammate of mine said when she found out about my dad's cancer, "Nicole, your dad *always* shows up and always has."

My dad was the best dad I could have ever asked for. It didn't start out easy, that's for sure. Before he and my mom got a divorce, we didn't have a very close relationship. After they separated, however, my dad became the hardest-working single dad I know. He made our lunches every single day. He coached us in sports and helped us with our homework. He taught us how to cook (even though we didn't always pay attention) and how to do the laundry. He came to every big life event that we celebrated, and he was always there with a shoulder to cry on and a box of tissues for the tough times. I'll never forget all the Michael Franti concerts he took me to and all the times he beat me at cards.

A very dear friend told me that she sees death as an exciting new journey for the soul, and I can't wait to see what that looks like for my dad. I know he'll be eating all the good food and seeing everything he didn't get to in this incarnation of life. I will miss him more than words will ever be able to convey, and at the same time, I know that he will never leave my side.

Thank you for always showing up, Papason. Thank you for being the best dad a girl could ever ask for. Thank you for loving me so unconditionally. Thank you for being my dad.

In Loving Memory

Brad Alan Dalby

January 2, 1960 – October 7, 2023

Section 5
Loving Myself

Time can be a difficult thing to capture on a page. There are so many parts and pieces to what happened in the first six months after Dad made his transition. I want to talk about them in a way that is healing and also relatable for those who may be going through something similar. I want people to connect with these chapters and feel inspired that, though they may feel like there's no way out, healing can happen.

Most of my notes from this time frame are breakthrough moments or epiphanies that came from certain events. They probably won't all be in chronological order, but I hope to share them in a way that will help bring some peace to a difficult phase of life that we all go through sooner or later.

No matter what you may be healing from right now, please know that you are loved.

Chapter 18

A Different Kind of Grief

I had never experienced this type of grief before. It was completely different from what I had gone through with Chase. And though I had lost loved ones in the past, I had never been this close to death. My dad was one of the most important people in my life, and to think that I would never see him again was more than just heartbreaking. It's one of the darkest feelings I've ever felt, and it wasn't simple. So many things were happening at one time, it made healing complex.

One of the pieces was figuring out how to fit into the world and talk to people about what was going on. As I said, over two hundred people showed up to Dad's celebration of life, and I couldn't tell you most of the conversations I had with them. My body went into survival mode, a functional freeze just to get through the day. Everyone showed up with such love and compassion, and at the same time, no one knew what to say any more than we as a family did.

That's the thing about grief—no one has the "right" thing to say. And it's not because we don't care. It's because we have no idea about the exact feelings someone is going through in that moment. We all feel different things from moment to moment, and one piece of advice that helped yesterday may send us spiraling today. For example, the hardest thing for me to hear was someone trying to relate because they had also lost their dad.

"I know how you feel because…"

"When my dad passed…"

"You're going to go through these phases, so make sure you…"

Again, it's not that these people didn't care about me— it was the opposite. They cared so much that they wanted to help me feel better. However, not even my brother knew what I felt. How could these people? I was the only person who knew what I needed in each moment, and the only thing I wanted was someone to simply be there with me.

My mom let me sit on the phone crying for hours, saying the same thing over and over again. Lyla would do the same while honoring every feeling I experienced. The friends who would open space and just let me cry made all the difference in the world. Some days, I wanted to do things with people, and others, I just needed space.

All of this to say that grief is a very lonely experience to a certain degree. I am unconditionally grateful for every soul in my world who shows up for me, and I will never take that for granted—and still, I'm the only one who knows what I need to process my dad's passing. It can feel very isolating.

One of the biggest things I've learned is that because we have no idea what someone else needs, the best way to be there for them is to simply be present. That might mean bringing a meal and leaving it on their doorstep, sending a message to say "Hi. I love you. I'm here," letting them cry, or simply listening. It sounds so simple, and yet, I think it's the most powerful way we can support someone who probably doesn't even know what they need in that moment.

I think it's also important to note that this feels contradictory to what most of us have been taught. We live in a culture that a) doesn't like to feel uncomfortable, and emotions make us uncomfortable, and b) wants to fix things that are perceived as broken. The marketing in our society wants us to believe that we lack something and, therefore, we need to fix it and fill the space where said thing is missing. Ads like "your feelings are valid," "you're enough exactly as you are," or "it's okay if you sit at home and process your emotions today" don't exist.

But what if that's why our society as a whole is becoming more depressed, anxious, and sick? What if, instead of covering up our grief and "moving on" with it, we found those safe spaces to express how we really feel so we can process and work through those emotions? Even when it makes us uncomfortable. Especially when it makes us uncomfortable.

"Emotions are energy in motion," and energy has to move. The more we avoid our feelings and tuck them away, the more stuck they become in our physical bodies until, eventually, our bodies become so sick and uncomfortable that we can no longer ignore its messages. They will whisper to us as long as they can until they have to start screaming to make us pay attention.

I've known this for some time now, but as humans, we are always a work in progress, and I guess I needed the reminder.

Chapter 19

I Can't Ignore It Anymore

To say that my plate was full from October 2023 through April 2024 is an understatement. My dad named me as the personal representative of the estate in his will. That didn't mean my brother couldn't help, however, most of the legal steps had to be executed by me. The hours I spent talking to attorneys, visiting courthouses and the DMV, closing bank accounts, selling multiple cars, managing and selling multiple homes, and communicating with insurance companies, the crematorium, and any other business involved equated to a full-time job. And it's not fun work in the slightest.

On top of that, I was still coaching fitness classes part-time, and I moved into a new apartment. The move was completely my choice, and it added a lot to my schedule, but I wasn't about to spend another holiday season in that home. As grateful as I was for the four years there, it had too many memories, good and bad.

As the cherry on top, Charlie (the kitten I'd had for six months) got so sick that I had to put him down two days before Dad passed away, and the following week, Chase and I said goodbye for the last time. My intuition had been telling me that the friendship was no longer healthy for either of us, and I finally made the choice to let go.

These heartbreaks may be unique to me, but how many times in life do we face mountains like this? It can be overwhelming when so much happens that is out of our control. Every one of us goes through heartbreak, loss, grief, and pain, but the world doesn't stop moving just because we face a challenge, as much as we would like it to. Each day, we get to decide to keep moving through these challenges or to hide under the covers and ignore our reality. And trust me, I feel the latter is a lot easier most days.

Instead of hiding under the covers from everything, I used to-do lists to keep me busy, floating above my grief. Christmastime came, and I put up a tree, like normal. I made plans to go see lights and attend the holiday fairs, like normal, and I expected to celebrate with friends and family, like normal. That was my way of coping with the train of life that doesn't stop.

To be fair, I knew I was overstimulated the night I started screaming at the universe because the gas light came on in my car, but I laughed it off and kept going. Just add it to the pile.

It wasn't until one day in the middle of December, when I had ignored everything long enough, that I couldn't hold onto the moving train anymore. That day, I didn't get out of bed until one thirty in the afternoon. My body had shut down. My mind went blank, and I was back in the space of not seeing a point to anything anymore. I was exhausted, overcome with grief, and so angry at the world for asking me to keep moving like nothing had happened. Why couldn't the world just stop and wait for me?

I've read that our breakdowns are actually breakthroughs, and after that day in December, I can agree. When you're at rock bottom, there's nowhere to go but up. I had no choice but to slow down and love myself enough to feel what was really going on—starting with compassion for myself and the fact that life wasn't normal anymore, so I didn't have to act like it was.

Allowing myself to listen to and understand that all my feelings were valid was one of the true starting points to this phase of my healing journey. First and foremost, Lyla helped me realize that it was okay to stay in bed until 1:30 p.m. without judging what I wasn't doing or getting done. I could forgive myself for judging myself, and in practicing that self-compassion, I could give myself the dignity to process everything. Then I started to reflect on what I had been covering up—all the thoughts about Dad's passing that I had shoved away as "unacceptable":

> He must be so relieved. He's free of his pain, of this world and all of its pain.

> Why are there so many cancer survivors and he wasn't one of them? Why the hell didn't he get to have a survivor story?

> I wish I were with him. He gets to be in a better place now. I'm stuck here.

> What's the point of being here anymore if he's not? We're all just going to die anyway.

> Everyone I know will eventually die. I can't go through this again.

> I saw the things that money and death can do to people. I wish they didn't exist.

> How can we all grieve so much at the same time? How are we supposed to support each other?

> Everyone's trying to tell me how to feel, and I hate it. I just have to have compassion for their grief and allow them to express themselves.

Most of these thoughts weren't happy, and I could skip this part of my story and tell you that "Time heals all things" and "We should have positive thoughts in difficult times."

But that wouldn't be the real story. That's not real life. We *do* have uncomfortable thoughts about life. We *do* wish things were different sometimes. And once we acknowledge those thoughts, we can process and move through them as part of our healing.

Chapter 20

Self-Love and Self-Acceptance

As I continued to feel these things and process my grief, I realized that I needed intentional self-acceptance for exactly how I was showing up. Acceptance for everything that I felt and compassion for it would allow it to move through me. If I were to judge any of my thoughts or emotions, I would no longer have permission to express what needed to come through. We tend to be our harshest critics, and with a world that already tries to tell us who to be, the last thing we should do is judge ourselves.

This meant becoming okay with the fact that I cried all the time, with or without people. I forgave myself for judging myself as lazy for not putting ornaments on my Christmas tree. I didn't beat myself up if I canceled plans with loved ones because I needed to take care of myself. I released any judgments of the days I didn't want to get out of bed. It was all showing up as part of me and my journey—even if I didn't want it to.

In February of 2024, I took a class through Mile Hi about mourning. It was an incredible class, and I fully believe anyone who has lost someone should have that type of experience/support. During its eight-week duration, one of the things we discussed was a theory that grief is like a string of fish. When you start to pull your fishing line out of the water, you'll find there are a lot more fish on that string than you thought. In other words, when you start to process your current grief, your past griefs come with it.

Chase was one of my big fish coming back up. I had done a lot of healing work right after everything had first happened in January of 2023, but I swept our last conversation in October under the rug with a lot of other things so I could survive what I had to get through. And besides, I had already been through the biggest heartbreak with him. This part should have been easy, right?

That was when I noticed that I had been shaming myself for loving Chase. Shame for loving him in the first place, for talking to him again after everything he had done, for thinking I could be with him again, and finally, most of all, for missing him more than I thought I ever could.

Some of this shame came from what I thought other people would say if they knew we had been talking again, from what their responses would be if I told them I had missed him terribly since we stopped talking in October, even though our relationship had exploded almost a year earlier. I didn't think a soul in the world would understand those feelings.

Then there was my shame because I wanted to be a stronger person. I had just lost my dad. Was I really going to let myself be upset over someone who clearly was not supposed to be in my life? How could I still feel love for him after he had said and done all those hurtful things? I had survived plenty of breakups in the past, and this one was the clearest cut.

However, the moment I decided all this shame was holding me back from healing, I became empowered to move forward. No matter my doubts about my past or what others think about my choices, I am the only one who gets to live my life. I am the one who gets to create a future of living in joy. And the only way I can do that is by letting go of my shame and loving myself for exactly who I am and where I am now.

And that person was a girl who missed Chase every day, missed her dad even more, who was emotionally and mentally exhausted and physically hurting from all the stress. It was time to start loving myself and every single tagalong that came with my messy journey.

So, I embraced the tears and difficult thoughts, started to share my boundaries with others, and followed my heart to guide me toward what I needed. One of those steps was to take a break from my job as a fitness coach. Though I loved the community where I worked more than any job I'd had in the past, it was time to give myself a break. And I wouldn't shame myself for stepping back in a society that believes our worth and value come from how productive we are in a professional career. I wouldn't allow myself to burn out for the sake of how others viewed me.

Through this self-love and acceptance, my world started to move in a different way, and I could celebrate again. Even if they weren't big wins, I wanted to make sure that I loved every up and down. For the first time in almost ten months, I began sleeping without a night-light. It was a small thing, and I loved myself for it.

Chapter 21

Coexisting Emotions

Our world is really good at separating people and things into categories—black or white, right or wrong, conservative or liberal, love or hate, good or bad. I even started to feel this as I worked deeper into my healing journey. I felt like I should either be sad or happy. I should be having a good day or an emotional day. I should be missing my dad or celebrating him. We use these labels to understand the world we live in; however, they limit our capacity not just to be ourselves but to grow as human beings.

As complex souls trying to find our authentic voices in a world of almost eight billion people, we need to feel multiple things at once. We may not know what to do with all of it, but our ability to tap into and validate all of our emotions and states of being gives us the freedom to work through any stuck energies we may have—to step out of the box we've placed ourselves in.

I had a lot of this coexisting energy coming up for me in the first six months of 2024. For example, I was both happy to be taking time off work and sad that I was leaving such an incredible community. My previous conditioning tried to convince me that this wasn't okay. If I made the decision to leave my job, then I shouldn't have the right to grieve it, right?

It's this mindset that I believe we and society can gaslight ourselves with—our emotions aren't valid if we've made a certain choice or if we can still celebrate. And so the cycle continues that we shove those feelings under a rug, and that's where they live until they manifest as physical pain, depression, and anxiety. We judge ourselves, and we assume others will do the same.

A prevalent example of this for me is the holidays. Father's Day and Dad's birthday have been two of the hardest so far, but I've noticed that no matter what the meaning is behind the holiday, I have struggled with them. My anxiety peaks. I become paralyzed in deciding what to do, and I get a pit in my stomach most of that day and the days that follow. I've opted out of going to numerous friend and family gatherings because I feel safer at home.

After I experienced this for the first few holidays following October, I tried to gaslight myself into ignoring those same emotions that came up on the Fourth of July. Sure, I have memories of spending a lot of Fourth of Julys with my dad, but the holiday's meaning has nothing to do with him. It should be an easy one to celebrate. Or so I thought. However, I still woke up with that anxiety that had come with every other holiday thus far. To say that I was frustrated and upset would be an understatement.

Instead of judging myself or trying to ignore my experience that morning, I sat with it for a while and listened to what my intuition was telling me. I had originally made plans to spend the day with a friend, and she was gracious enough to give me time and space to feel what was coming. What came from that space was something of an epiphany—I think the reason I have such anxiety around holidays is because, in a world that is constantly changing, that looks different from day to day and year to year, holidays are a constant. They happen every year, no matter what, and not only did I remember every holiday I had spent with Dad, but they also reminded me that he would never be here for another one. The loss after celebrating thirty-four years of holidays with him in the world is huge.

This deep realization brought me both relief and sorrow. Thank goodness this was one of the moments I could call my mom and just cry. I explained to her what I felt and that I didn't have an answer, and all she said was "These days happen." We didn't try to change or fix it. We just allowed ourselves to feel. It took a few days and passing on a few gatherings to let these emotions move through again. I managed to spend some time with my friend at the pool, and on the night of the Fourth of July, I came home to sit on the balcony in my pajamas and watch the fireworks with my cat, Claire. I smiled at the beauty and cried that Dad wasn't there. Both things were true, and I allowed them to be present.

Opening the doors and allowing myself to feel everything like the holidays without the need to fix it has been a freeing experience. Another example is the multiple emotions I felt for Chase at the beginning of the year. I missed him, and I was so angry at him, and I still kept wanting to talk to him. I was dumbfounded that I could still love him. Fifty contradicting emotions simultaneously existed in one soul.

Outside my feelings for Dad and Chase, I constantly experience this emotional paradox in my everyday life. Some days, I have no fear of what could happen to me because I've already experienced the worst, and simultaneously, I'll be extremely anxious that the next phone call I receive will be more bad news. At one point, my compassion for grumpy people skyrocketed because I wanted to be one of them. I wanted to be so mad at the pain this world holds and not care about anyone, and at the same time, I still felt grateful for the life I had been given and the space I was creating.

Most importantly—none of this is wrong. None of these feelings are invalid, less than real, or unimportant. Our feelings are gifts that show us where we are in our journey, and allowing multiple things to be true at once, without judgment, is freedom. I experienced that freedom after traveling to North Carolina to visit a dear friend. Traveling was something I had been afraid of doing since Dad passed away, which is out of character for me. It's always been one of my greatest passions. But I didn't feel safe, and I didn't want to travel without Dad in the world.

I knew that this trip to North Carolina would be a safe space for me with good people, and I had lived with this friend after college, so she knew me well. There were no expectations of showing up a certain way, and the trip was incredible. Simultaneously, however, my heart ached for how much I missed Dad the entire time. Shouldn't I be able to have one weekend of fun without thinking about him so much?

After talking it through with Lyla, I realized that a time may never come when I don't miss my dad. He will always be a part of my life, and I don't have to push that away. I can miss him dearly and be sad that he's gone while learning to enjoy traveling in a new way, with his spirit. I'm allowed to go out and enjoy myself with friends and make sure I bring the tissues in case the grief hits suddenly.

I'm allowed to feel and express it all. We all are.

Chapter 22

The Physical Body

I want to end this section with a note on the healing of my physical body because it's been a huge part of this journey, and many of us face challenges with how our pain manifests. Since I injured my back and had norovirus at the beginning of 2023, my body has yet to return to fully pain free. In September 2023, I had lower back surgery to remove multiple lipomas (fatty tissues) that we thought were causing most of my pain, and it helped tremendously. The lower back pain that I had experienced since I was in a car wreck in 2015 was ninety percent gone.

One spot, however, on my SI joint, kept flaring up. I worked with two different physical therapists, a functional range conditioning specialist, massage therapy, chiropractic care, and acupuncture, and this spot hung on like a nagging fly. Not to mention the emotional stress of Dad's passing did not create an easy healing environment for my body.

The pain slowly moved to the front of my hip joint, and I decided to get some imaging done to make sure it wasn't something more serious.

The MRI showed what's known as a hip impingement with a partial hip labrum tear—basically, the femur is misshapen and is tearing the labrum. After trying a steroid injection that did more harm than good, I talked to two different surgeons about what surgery would look like. It's microscopic, however, the recovery is intense for someone who wanted to spend all summer being active outside. Deciding between that and managing the pain felt like an unfair decision that I didn't want to make.

I was explaining that frustration to Lyla one day, and she made an incredible point, as she always does.

"Nicole, it seems like you're looking outside of yourself for your healing. What if you just told your body that you trust her to know exactly what she needs?"

So, that's exactly what I did.

I sat down to meditate, and I spoke directly to my body, affirming the same thing over and over. "I trust you. I love you. I know you know exactly what we need."

I completely surrendered to Spirit and my body's guidance. If I was meant to have surgery, then I would make it work. If I could heal without surgery, I knew that I would be guided in the right direction to do so. By not trying to force the decision anymore, I removed my attachment to the outcome so I could let my higher self show me what to do next. Either way would be the right path as long as I trusted in my guidance.

The next day, at acupuncture, I was explaining the situation to Ashlie. She happened to know another chiropractor who adjusted in a way that she thought would help my hip. Willing to try anything at this point, I trusted the breadcrumbs and made an appointment.

Not only did this chiropractor explain my X-rays to me more thoroughly than anyone had before, but she told me that she believed if we could get my body back into alignment and create space, my hip would have room to heal itself. She was speaking my language, and for the first time in a while, I felt truly heard and understood when it came to my physical body. I had a clearer idea of why I was experiencing the pain, and she was willing to walk with me through the healing process.

After a month of seeing her several times a week, I was able to start biking and hiking longer distances again. I even completed a "Triple Soul-Pass" event, during which I hiked the Manitou Incline, cycled eighteen miles to and from Boulder, and cycled 12.6 miles around Washington Park to remember my dad and raise money for three different charities near to my heart. It was my version of a "comeback event," and it was freedom.

Because I've been able to heal in this way, I've made it my goal to hike and bike as many miles as I can this summer. It's been my way of processing and moving through my body and my emotions. As a holistic health coach, I know that emotions can play a huge role in physical pain. Many wisdom seekers tell us our bodies perceive physical pain as an easier experience than breaking down and vulnerably sharing our emotions with the world.

The piece that I'm still figuring out is how much of my hip is related to these emotions and how much of it is mechanical. However, now I know that I can't force that answer. My job is to keep trusting my body and giving myself the grace I need to experience the answers.

This included changing the expectations I had for myself and my fitness level. For the first few months of my injuries, I was solely focused on getting back to where I was before. I was determined to heal so I could return to my HIIT classes four days a week, moving just as fast and lifting just as much. Like so many of us do, I was "getting back on track."

But what if that track no longer serves us? What if we aren't on a specific track but rather pathways that take us somewhere better than where we've been if we're willing to trust? By putting the pressure on ourselves to get back to a certain place, I believe we limit our potential to experience what is currently waiting for us. It probably looks different than we thought it would, and we may need to grieve that piece of life we had, for it is still a loss. However, what is waiting may be a far greater outcome than we thought possible because we were trying to fit it into the only way we had experienced life so far.

When I shifted my mindset from "I need to heal to get back to where I was" to "My only job right now is to listen to what my body needs, trust her, and heal my hip," I could breathe again. I was allowing my body to speak and tell me what she needed with permission and without judgment. Even when that meant slowing down, changing my movement patterns, and trying things I had deemed as "not worth my time" in the past.

This grace and presence for my body, continual love and self-care, along with chiropractic work and acupuncture have progressed my pain from a constant eight or nine, on a scale of ten, to a four or five on an average day. I am so grateful that I can move and do the things I love to do. Movement truly is medicine. I plan to continue holding this space for my hip and any other physical discomfort that comes up, hopefully avoiding surgery altogether. However, I also know that because I trust my body and my higher self, I can detach from the outcome, whatever that may be, and know that I am safe on whichever path comes next.

Section 6
Where Do I Go From Here?

When we realize that the gift of life is the journey and not the destination, I think we are free to fully live. I have no idea where my next adventure will take me, but I know that I don't want to try and control it. I want to surrender fully to the beautiful mess that continues to unfold for me.

I am walking into this next phase of my journey as a new person, with new lessons and new realizations of who I am and what I stand for. The following chapters summarize the shift I've experienced as a human being, the epiphanies I want to continue to carry with me, and how I will continue to share my dad's story.

Life continues, and so do we.

Chapter 23

COCO

May of 2024 came with another shift. The last items of Dad's estate had been settled. The weather was getting warmer. The days were getting longer, and I was starting to create again. Because I no longer had as many demands on my time, I had the capacity to dream what I wanted to dream about. I started sharing motivational messages, I picked up this book and continued my writing, and it seemed like life outside my grief started to poke up its head every now and then.

One of those pokes would become one of the biggest transformations I've ever experienced. Jon Hillstead led an expansion retreat in Sedona, Arizona, and I decided to go. Thirteen of us did, including Jon and his co-facilitator, Katie. We came from all across the world for five days to expand through hiking in the vortex, breath work, sound healing, and soul-connected conversations, which led to numerous breakthroughs.

My biggest breakthrough happened in a small kiva on the retreat center property. We had all hiked that morning, and I had been struggling to express something that I felt was stuck in my throat—a sound, a word, a scream. I couldn't tell what it was, and I couldn't shake the feeling that I needed to express myself somehow.

After we returned from our hike, Jon told me about a little kiva on the lawn out back. He suggested that I go down there and scream and yell and let it all go to try releasing that calling. I didn't think it would hurt, so I followed him and Katie down to the small, round hut and sat with my feet in the dirt to feel what came forth.

Jon grabbed a sound bowl and started to play while Katie used her voice to harmonize with it. I stood and did the same, but quite honestly, I felt a little self-conscious about trying to make my voice match the melodic hertz of the bowl.

Right as I thought this, Katie said, "Nicole, don't think about it. Just let it flow, no matter what it sounds like."

That was the permission I needed to fully express my feelings. What sounded like gibberish, and I would later learn was light language, started flowing from my voice. I spoke the sounds, but they weren't from my logical mind. They came from my soul, my higher self. I fully let go of preconceived judgments and spoke my truth in that moment.

Once the sound bowl stopped, we all quieted our voices and sat for a minute.

"How do you feel now?" Katie asked.

The question felt loaded. "It feels like I have a firecracker that wants to explode from my throat. Like we've just lit a spark that needs to burst." I paused for a moment, then I continued. "I also feel like my dad is here, *screaming* at me that he is here. Like he's not going anywhere. Honestly, I've been so afraid to talk about him on this trip because I don't know these people. Everyone has expectations for how I should handle this whole thing, and I feel like, when I lost my dad, I lost a huge piece of my voice. But he's been showing up for me everywhere during this retreat, and I can't ignore him anymore."

It was true. My dad had brought me a dozen signs a day that he was there with me.

"You have to process and feel everything in your own time," Jon said.

I knew that, but it's always comforting when someone reinforces it.

At that point, another one of the retreat participants had joined us in the kiva, and I knew I needed to process more. Katie and Jon both gave me a hug, and Katie told me to take the time to do whatever I needed to for the next hour or so.

I awkwardly walked to the front lawn, where I paused for a minute, thinking that I would sit and meditate. I stood back up, feeling anxious, and kept walking up the hill to the house where I was staying. The tears had already started streaming down my face, and I knew I would lose it the minute I was safe inside the house.

None of my housemates were there, and for that, I am grateful because I shut the door, dropped to the floor, and started to scream—a scream like I had never made before. I screamed about the anger I felt over losing my dad. I screamed about how unfair the world is and how much pain I had endured over the last sixteen months. I screamed for the things I had wanted to say my whole life and hadn't because of how I was expected to show up in the world. Then I screamed just for the sake of being heard.

The screams turned to uncontrollable sobs that I didn't think would ever stop. I hyperventilated until I thought I would pass out, banged on the floor in fits of rage and agony, pulled at my clothes to get out of the discomfort of this human life.

Then, it stopped.

As suddenly as it had started.

And not only did it stop, but it took a weight from my soul that I had carried for longer than I could remember. Not just the grief from the recent months, but from my entire life. The stifled voice that had been inside me since I was a kid was free. I was free.

For the next hour, I walked around the house, speaking light language, singing in the shower, laughing until I cried again, dancing in my room. Simply being free. I had shed the layers of me that no longer served a purpose, and I had stepped into a new version of myself. A lighter version, a louder version, a brighter version.

Not only did that experience change me, but that group of thirteen individuals supported me in such a way that I can never express enough gratitude for them. They allowed me to speak my truth, sing and yell on the trails, tell my story, and live as my authentic self. One of the brightest souls there even reminded me that making a mess with glitter is completely acceptable and should be encouraged if that's how you shine brighter in this world.

Her name is Julianna, and I think the world should aspire to shine as brightly as she does. Covered in glitter and hiking in bedazzled shoes, she reminded me that it doesn't matter what anyone thinks of you as long as you live as your truest self. That's the light we all need to give to each other. That's the light that will help this world heal.

On the first night of the retreat, Julianna gave me the nickname "Coco." It resonated with me for so many reasons, and that's the name I started yelling on the hiking trails.

"Coco loooooooooooooooooo!"

This is my expression and my call whenever I want to share my freedom with the world.

Coco isn't just a nickname anymore. It's the girl who came home with a voice. It's the girl who talks freely about her dad and shares his story. It's the girl who shines brighter even when others don't agree with her words. It's the girl who dances more and wears glitter out in public. Coco is the small child who came out to be loud again. Coco is free.

I am free.

Chapter 24

The Dark Night of the Soul

I came home from Sedona on a cloud. It was one of those experiences I couldn't really talk about when people asked, because there weren't words to convey the gravity of what I had gone through. And if you weren't there, it would be hard to understand such a spiritual transformation. This is also known as the integration process—working to integrate my new self and what I had experienced into the life I had been living before.

Some of that came easy, and some of it challenged me to my limits. People expect you to come back as the same person, and you have to lovingly show them you aren't that person anymore. Yes, I was still living this life, but I had new boundaries and passions and a new voice that I would not lose again.

It's also my belief that as we level up in our personal-growth journeys, Spirit will challenge us with new experiences to break us into our higher selves. Once we've asked for that deeper, connected, and passion-led life, Spirit will respond by offering us ways to grow into that new space. And if you've ever seen a plant grow out of a seed, ugly destruction occurs before it breaks free.

One such destruction happened a couple of weeks after I got home. I had been in the middle of a legal wage dispute for almost two years. After eight months of investigation, the state had awarded me the case. The other party, however, appealed the state's decision, and we sat through a hearing with a judge to determine whether or not the appeal would be granted. Both attorneys I worked with were certain it was a clear-cut case. The facts were concrete, and there was no way the judge would grant the appeal.

In the brief that the judge sent, they did, indeed, disagree with almost everything that the other party had stated in the hearing. In summary, several examples were given that proved they had not shown any reason for the decision to be appealed, and their arguments did not have validity. This was comforting to know that the state had made the right decision.

As I read to the bottom of the document, however, the judge ultimately decided to grant the appeal and reverse the state's decision. The other party was off the hook for anything they had owed. The case was dropped.

To say that I was shocked would be an understatement. This was such a straightforward case. The words on the page even stated so. My logical brain couldn't make sense of what had just happened, and the attorney I was working with agreed. Here was another legal decision that didn't seem fair or justified. How could those kinds of people get away with such unkind actions?

These thoughts kept me up for three nights in a row. I knew I could find a deeper lesson in all of it, but I couldn't see it, and my brain wanted these people to be held accountable for their mistakes. It was at 2 a.m. on the third night of no sleep that I was called to watch a video from Reverend Josh Reeves, one of the colead ministers at Mile Hi Church. I was scrolling through the church website, and his video called "The Dark Night of the Soul" jumped out at me.

He started by discussing the journey of a soul and how part of that journey sometimes goes through the darkness of night. A place with no stars, no light—a place of unknowing and, at the same time, immense possibility. It could be a time of loss or betrayal or a feeling of unworthiness that Josh describes as a "breaking open" of the soul.

Instead of looking at this as a punishment or a challenge from God, Josh invited us to ask in these dark times, "What am I being initiated into right now?" He continued to say that instead of blaming ourselves in these dark times, we can have faith in the potential of what is being asked of us.

He explained, "We can say, 'I have set an intention

to live in a greater way, and my life is responding to me through this change, through this loss...' The pain can be teaching us what we need to know to step into our next level of becoming."

Josh finished by sharing that the Dark Night of the Soul is a spiritual practice of having faith in the unknown—being in the dark, sitting with it, and having faith in what we don't know. If we knew the reason for it all or what would happen next, we might try to control it or not even take the next steps of our journey.

I watched that video four times that night.

It was the recent legal dispute. It was losing my dad. It was my physical injuries. It was saying goodbye to Chase. It was every heartbreak I'd been through in life—the Dark Night of the Soul was every challenge that I had faced, and they were all initiating me into the next phase of my journey. I had set the intention to live in a greater way, and life was showing me what I needed to know to step into my next level with the pain from all these challenges. I didn't need to know the why. I could trust that the ripple effect of each of these moments held the highest and greatest good for everyone involved, even if I couldn't see it. I could have faith in the unknown.

I am so grateful to Josh for this message. It came at the perfect time. It was the love my heart needed in that moment, and the next evening, I slept for ten hours straight.

Chapter 25

Regulating the Nervous System

Physical, mental, emotional, and spiritual healing were all forms I was familiar with prior to 2023. I had spent some time processing each of them, depending on the phase of my journey, and I believe they are nonexclusive to each other when it comes to self-growth. When you work on healing one, the others transform in some way. The category unfamiliar to me was healing, or regulating, the nervous system.

My research in this area started after the incident with Chase and continued after Dad passed away. Spiritual coaching, acupuncture, and chiropractic care helped tremendously, and at the same time, my digestive system was still a mess. It took me anywhere from one to three hours to fall asleep at night, and crowds of more than three or four people made me so uncomfortable that my favorite place to be was at home, cuddling with my cat, Claire. As a health coach, I had learned these were all signs that my body was living in the sympathetic (fight-or-flight) response, and I wanted to learn ways to calm myself into the parasympathetic nervous system (rest and digest).

From everything I have read, many of us in today's culture live constantly in that sympathetic nervous system because of stress, trauma, and toxins in our environment. We developed this response as hunters and gatherers when we were being chased by animals that wanted to eat us. Our bodies learned three different survival techniques in this situation—fight, flight, or freeze and fawn. If we couldn't fight the animal that was chasing us, we would try to run from it. If we weren't fast enough to run, we would freeze and play dead in hopes they would leave us alone.

These survival modes are still the prevalent ways in which we cope with stress, but our stressors have evolved from being chased every now and then to being stimulated, upset, and anxious multiple times throughout the day. As a result, our body is constantly going into a hyperarousal (fight-or-flight) state, where we are anxious, irritable, tense, and panicked, or hypoarousal (freeze-or-fawn) state, where we are depressed, numb, disassociated, hopeless, and exhausted. In both scenarios, most of our bodily functions can't work properly because they are focused on keeping us alive and safe. In other words, we are in survival mode. This survival mode is also the response we experience after any type of trauma. Our brains constantly wonder if something bad will happen again, and our nervous system tries to prevent that from occurring, so we become stuck. Our thoughts and actions are at odds, attempting to prevent another trauma, and therefore, our other systems are handicapped. This is exhausting both physically and mentally because all our fuel is used to survive, even if the threat is only perceived or hasn't actually occurred.

I've also learned that trying to change your thoughts to positive thinking won't necessarily help calm your nervous system, because the equivalent of one hundred lanes run between the body and the brain on their highway of communication, also known as the vagus nerve, and only twenty of those carry information from the brain to the body. The other eighty transport information in the opposite direction, from the body to the brain. Telling someone to "just get over it" in this scenario isn't helpful because our brains need a different type of attention and our bodies are actually running the show. Regulating this system is all about feeling safe in our environment and safe in our body so it can send signals to the brain to calm down.

Thankfully, there are many different ways to do this, and the trick is learning the ones that work best for you. One of the most transformational steps I have taken to regulate my nervous system is to honor exactly what my body asks for. If I don't feel safe going out in public, I stay home. If I am exhausted when I wake up, I fall back asleep for a while. If my clothes don't fit just right, I change into some-thing more comfortable, even if it isn't stylish (I still wear the same five T-shirts almost every week). By demonstrating to myself that I will listen to what I need and honor it, my intuition feels safer simply existing in the world because she knows she will be understood.

This has also led me down the path of setting more boundaries with the people I interact with. After almost thirty-five years of people pleasing, the last year has taught me that when I do things out of obligation, I negate what my body is asking from me, which sends a signal that her needs don't matter. Saying no to others doesn't mean I am not compassionate, and I can still love my family and friends fiercely while listening to my heart when she doesn't want to do something. In turn, I'm reaffirming with my nervous system that my choices matter and I am safe choosing what is right for me, even when others don't understand.

Another choice I've made in this healing process is to stop drinking alcohol. This choice was inspired by the soul family that I went to Sedona with. A month before our trip, we had a pre-retreat Zoom call, and I happened to be hun-gover that morning (not from a crazy party, but from two drinks the night before). My body has told me for a while now that she doesn't feel well after I drink, and so I decided to detox for thirty days before Sedona to get clear for the experience. While I was there, a few of the retreat partic-ipants shared their sober stories with me. I talked with a housemate who is a homeopath about why my body craves alcohol, and ultimately, I decided to not start drinking again when I got home. It was a hard decision at first, but I feel better without drinking, my nervous system can regulate easier, and my intuition is clearer—all things that help calm anxiety.

I do want to make a note here about a conversation I recently had with a dear friend of mine, Jami. We went out to dinner together, and the day before our meeting was particularly difficult for me. My nervous system had completely shut down again—I had a hard time getting off the floor or even talking for close to forty minutes. When I explained this to Jami and told her how frustrated I was that after all the healing work I've done, I still have moments like this, she had the perfect response.

"Nicole, you've got to remember that when we remove coping mechanisms like alcohol, reckless sex, overscheduling, people pleasing, or working too much, our nervous systems have a greater ability to feel emotions and might end up feeling them harder. That's why we do the work to teach ourselves how to cope with those feelings in a different way. Now that you aren't ignoring yourself, these emotions have space to come up and move through your system instead of getting stuck as physical illness."

This was such an important realization for me, and I am so grateful that Jami reminded me to give myself grace. Our bodies take time to learn new skills, and when we've been conditioned to cope a certain way our entire lives, redirecting our habits requires patience. I have opened new pathways of self-healing and regulating that seem harder some days, but in the end, I know I am creating a deeper sense of security for myself.

Other practices that have helped me feel safer are decluttering my home (every inch of it), sleeping (sometimes ten hours a night), meditation, yoga, walking in the sunshine, being in nature and aligning with the earth's frequencies, cold plunges (and even cold exposure in the snow), saunas, talking to people I trust, physical movement (hiking, biking, and dancing), cuddles with Claire, and breathing. Breathing is such a simple technique available to us all, and yet, it's usually the last thing we pay attention to throughout the day. If we simply exhale for a little longer than we inhale and slow our breath, we can tell the brain we are safe.

This is just a small list of the different ways to help reregulate our nervous system in such a fast-paced society, and I'm still experimenting with what works for me during different phases of life. Healing is not a linear journey, and I have plenty of days when I collapse and feel as though I am back at square one. My body will shut down, I won't sleep, or I'll feel frozen and withdrawn. In those moments, I try to remember it's all a part of the journey and, sometimes, my body just needs to express her frustrations to move through them. Sometimes, fixing and analyzing aren't the best answers. Rather, our bodies just need to feel and express.

I encourage anyone reading this to find one or two simple ways to experiment with reregulating your nervous system. I believe more research will come about this type cf healing, and I also believe it will help us change the way we interact with the world for the better.

Chapter 26

A Spiral Worker

Eleven years ago, I was hiking, and when I reached the top of the trail, I sat down to meditate. I wasn't trying to focus on anything specific but, instead, be present and aware of what was coming up for me. In that moment, I kept seeing a spiral spinning on the back of my eyelids. I thought it was the sunlight at first, but even when I turned the other way, it was still there.

I didn't think much of it then, but ever since that hike, I have been drawn to spirals every time I see them in the world—in nature, on clothing, in paintings or artwork. My fascination with them has morphed from a mere pleasure in their design to a connection with how they represent the flow of nature and water, then to my current and strongest belief that it is a symbol of my calling and passion in this life—to be a spiral worker and bring light to the beauty in what our world sees as two or more extremes. It is said that there are lightworkers among us, whose souls come to this planet to help others and bring light to our society. These are people who help and serve others and have the purpose of empowering hope in tough times. I love this idea, and I also believe I am meant to help others embrace the dark. We cannot have one without the other.

One of the most prevalent examples of two extremes I currently experience on my healing journey is the juxtaposition between what I call the "get over it" and the mindset of victimhood. Much of our society is torn between these two lifestyles. Some believe we shouldn't share our emotions or stories with the world because crying is too vulnerable and if we just change our thinking and "rub some dirt on it," our problems will go away and we can fast-forward through our pain. In the spiritual sense, this can also turn into spiritual bypassing, where we affirm that everything is working for our good and, therefore, bypass how the pain needs to be felt.

Those on the other side of the spectrum carry their traumas and hurts for their entire lives, allowing them to shape who they become and create their identity in the world. The world has hurt them so much that they get stuck in the sorrows of life. To them, the former group of people is considered insensitive, and reversely, those in the get-over-it mindset say that the latter group just needs to exercise, eat healthy, and move on with their lives.

My theory is—what about both? What if a grounded

and connected space exists between these two lifestyles? What if we can find the best of both and spiral them together to create the most supportive healing experience of all? Yes, it's important to do the work to heal and move through our pain, but it's also beneficial to allow ourselves the space to feel and express and grieve. At the same time, as we grieve and feel every emotion, I think it's important to not get stuck there or let it rule the rest of our lives. A colorful palette sits between these black and white spaces and allows for the most authentic version of self-expression.

I feel like my entire being exists in this spiral most days. Some moments, I can step back and see the beauty in the world and be grateful for it all, and other days, a panic attack surfaces because I am so afraid of what will happen next. Some days, I feel leaps and bounds better after a six-mile hike in the sunshine, and other days, all my body needs is a nap on the couch and a good book with nothing to do. There is a balance between fixing and feeling, and I believe that it takes a new type of living and realization to authentically grow into a coexistence of both.

That's what the spiral does for me right now. It helps me create my new, flexible self that is not so rigid. This self is sometimes afraid to be in the world, however, it is also the most authentic version of me yet. This new self realizes that I loved Chase so much because he was one of the first people to love me fully as I started to express my authentic voice, and at the same time, he was also what some people call a "twin flame"—a person who mirrors the areas in us with the most growth potential. I felt a deep connection with and love for him, and that experience showed me where I can work on myself.

This new self also accepts that there are moments when I can celebrate my life with my dad, talk to him, and dance about all the great memories we have together. At the same time, I still wake up many days with overwhelming grief because I will never get to hug my dad again. He will never meet my future partner or family, and he won't be in my physical world. The spiral of these two deep emotions forms me into a new and more compassionate human being who can allow it all to show up when it needs to.

On a more global scale, I realize that this spiral could work to heal the relationships we have with each other. Instead of blaming our parents for the childhood trauma they may have enabled, on the one hand, or allowing their traditions to dictate our futures, on the other, what if we could have compassion for where they came from and the fact that they did the best with what they had, while also taking responsibility to set our new boundaries and communicate them with love to one another? Instead of pitting the "wrongs" of certain religions against the "wrongs" of certain lifestyles, what if we found the truth and love in both and came to share those goods? Instead of having to choose conservative or liberal in every detail, what if we realized the good in both and highlighted it to help compromise our differences? Why can't both Eastern and Western medicine have correct information and resources for our physical bodies?

I don't believe the world has to exist in black and white. I believe we can exist in this colorful spiral where each extreme has its truth, and those truths can come together to create an out-of-the-box, more authentic experience that allows for grace and forgiveness in all that it means to be human. We will never be able to live fully if we hold ourselves to these rigid truths that only birth what already exists. A new version of ourselves is waiting to express itself if we can step away from the concrete rules we've always known and allow the unknown to come alive.

Chapter 27

Check out the Moon, Champ!

When my dad was first diagnosed with cancer, I remember telling him that he would beat it and, someday, he and I would stand on stage and tell our stories together. We would share with the world how we both beat the odds of heartbreak and disease, and we were the walking miracles that every human on Earth had the potential to be. Our stories would inspire others to live life as fully as possible.

Well, it may look a little different than I thought it would, but I will always keep that promise to my dad. I will continue to share our stories with the world in the hope that we can be the inspiration that someone needs to keep going or the reason that someone lives more authentically and true to themselves. It's not just a cliché when they say life is short. Losing someone so suddenly reminds us how important it is to take advantage of today.

My dad is with me now more than ever. He shows up fifty times a day to guide me in the right direction or listen to me talk about the world. He laughs with me when I tell him what's going on with our family or what latest curiosity Claire's gotten into. I can even feel him holding space for me when I sit on the kitchen floor crying and screaming at him because I am mad that he left so soon. The stories I could share about my dad since he passed could fill an entire book. Here are just a few of the ones that stick out most.

One of the important things my dad did after making his transition was to bring some of my dearest friends back into my life. As time passes and lives change, friendships transition, and we lose touch with people who will always be part of our hearts. Some of those people who I hadn't talked to in months or years came to my dad's celebration of life. To see them sitting in those seats, supporting me and my family overwhelmed me to my core. Just the fact that they showed up was priceless, and it's led to some of us refreshing our relationships.

Gina and Sinjin are two such friends, and for a couple of months in a row, after the holidays were over, we met for dinner to catch up on where our lives had taken us the past few years. I've known Gina since the third grade, and Sinjin since middle school, and we have been through hell and back, together and apart. They both knew my dad well, which comforted me because we could share stories about the things we'd all done together when he was alive.

We've also shared lessons that Dad still teaches us to this day. I shared, for example, that losing him so soon has taught me that I never want to keep something on my heart from someone important to me. You never know if the chance to say it will pass you by, and I've written several letters to family and friends with things that I've wanted to say but have held back because of fear or doubt or I just simply thought I would always have time. Now, I realize that I might not have the opportunity to tell them tomorrow, and I want to make sure that I've expressed my love or gratitude or connection with them today.

Sinjin shared that Dad's passing made him take a second look at his life and ask if he was truly living in the now. My dad worked for over forty years to save money for retirement, but he also started to travel and experience the things he really wanted to in the last few years of his life. He didn't wait until his retirement to start living, and Sinjin realized he didn't want to either.

The waterworks really began when Gina shared her story. She is an elementary school teacher (bless her), and one of the exercises that she does with her students every week is to have them write down their highs and lows— what is something great that happened that week, and what is something not so great. I didn't remember this, but Gina reminded me that she got the idea from my dad. When he and my mom first got divorced and he had majority custody during the school year, he would ask me and my brother and any friends who came for dinner what our highs and lows were from that day. It was his way of connecting with us awkward preteens, especially before he and my brother got to a better place in their relationship.

As kids, it didn't seem like a big deal, but Gina explained, "It may sound silly, but that simple exercise that your dad taught us has saved some of my students' lives. I get to know them more and hear the good they experience, but I've also had moments when a student will share something serious that they haven't shared with anyone else, and I've had to intervene. It has changed lives."

We never know the seeds that we plant and the lives that we continue to touch by simply living this life with the people around us. Many loved ones have shared stories with me about my dad and what they remember about him. Those memories will never fade for those of us whose lives he impacted, even if he didn't know he was doing it.

Not only does he show up for me in the memories of those who loved him, but he also gives me the gift of fulfilling the last request I asked him for.

Once it was clear that he would not be with us for much longer, I said, "Dad, I hope you come back next year as a million butterflies."

He gave me a big hug and smiled with tears in his eyes.

Not only did he listen to my request, but he's gone above and beyond. I've been surrounded by more butterflies while hiking this year than I've ever seen before. Just today, I was at the top of a new trail I've been exploring, and at least a dozen butterflies were chasing each other and fluttering around in the sunshine.

When I commented on how amazing they were to a few hikers standing with me, one of the gentlemen said, "Yeah, it's really incredible! We've seen so many this year. It's the year of the butterflies!"

Leave it to my dad to be my biggest cheerleader and come back as a year of butterflies.

Some days, his energy is so loud and present that I'm convinced his soul transformed into his loudest and most authentic voice in this new phase of his journey. He has guided me to the best parking spots in the middle of downtown construction, when I didn't want to go to the theater without him in the first place. He's asked me to stop mid-bike ride, breathe in the sunshine, and call in compassion for the people I thought I couldn't forgive in the legal wage dispute. He guided me to find the most perfect apartment with a view of the sunset right on a golf course. He ensured every step of my grandparents' move (after thirty-eight years in the same house) fell smoothly into place. He shows up in songs, messages at church, T-shirts, nature, and books that I'm reading. And he still sits with me when I go to one of his favorite restaurants for dinner by myself—the place where he once sat across the table from me during my deepest depression after Chase, having no clue what to say but knowing that I needed to be with someone.

I'll continue to watch for and expect these miracles for the rest of my life. He's taught me that I don't have to carry physical objects from him to guarantee his presence. While dancing outside, I even lost the ring he gave me twenty years ago, and three days later (after my mom had helped me come to terms with the fact that he would rather I dance than worry about an object), I found the ring in the grass along the street. His energy is truly a miracle, and it is always with me. I'll continue to celebrate his memory by fundraising for charities that meant something to him, buying doughnuts for the congregation at church because that's how he bribed me to go on Sundays as a kid, and I'll probably keep getting tattoos that remind me of him.

The tattoo I recently got on my back, for example, was designed before my dad found out about his cancer. It's an eagle flying across the moon. After my dad was gone, it could not have been clearer as to why the artist had been guided to add the moon to the background months earlier—my dad used to text or call me all the time when the moon was full and say, "Check out the moon, Champ!"

Every time the moon is out now, I say hi to Dad.

Chapter 28

The Courage to Heal

As I continue to live this journey of life and learn the lessons that keep coming, I realize that this book could continue forever. I fear ending it because there is still so much I haven't said about my healing over the past eighteen months. What if I forgot to share something big that could help someone on their path? How do I share next week's lessons with the world and the ones that come the week after that? It's a never-ending adventure, and I want to make sure I've shared enough of my story to help someone else.

But this isn't the end. Whether it's another book, sharing through social media, speaking in public, or simply sitting with a friend who needs someone to listen, I know that my story doesn't end here. Just like my dad's story continues, so will mine. Just as life doesn't stop for pain, it doesn't stop unfolding the beauty that is yet to reveal itself either. I can sit here and analyze the river and try to plan the "perfect" timing, or I can jump in the water and splash through life as it flows.

I do know a few things for certain. Grief isn't linear, and it doesn't unfold in steps that always resolve themselves. It's a circle that can restart and throw us back to the beginning at any time. I am still amazed by the fact that I can be having a great day, or a great week, feeling like I'm getting back into a routine again and building my life back up, and maybe something will trigger it, or simply out of nowhere, I'll break down crying and be paralyzed for the rest of the week. The day that I finished the first draft of this book, for example, I was overcome with a fresh wave of grief. Writing this book has been one of the distractions from my grief, and now I wonder what I'll do next. It's another unknown void that's somewhat scary and reopens the wound.

We can't force this to go away, and I believe we need to be gentle with ourselves when it shows up again and again. Grief doesn't leave us—we simply get stronger from living with it. Some people compare grief to a stone we carry in our pockets that never gets smaller, but we get stronger in carrying it. I think of it more like a hole in the ground, or our hearts. Depending on the grief we experience, the holes will vary in size, and they never get filled. However, every time we do the work to heal, we plant new flowers and grow new life around the opening. Eventually, it becomes a beautiful reminder that allows light to enter, never disappearing but a little softer than it was when it was first dug. Each time a fresh wave of grief comes over us, we have more tools and experience to navigate the unknown. I know I am becoming more comfortable in the world, and yet, the majority of the time, I still feel safest at home, with Claire, on the couch, or hiking in the mountains with no one around.

I know that healing takes time and is unpredictable. There is a scene from the Disney movie *Tangled* when Rapunzel has just escaped her tower, and she debates with herself whether she's made the right decision or not. I see this as the healing journey—one moment we know we are on the right path and we'll be okay, and thirty seconds later, we want to crawl back into a hole and never come out because we don't know if the world will ever be bright again.

If we can allow all these things to be true at once, allow them to coexist and express ourselves through emotions that come with them, our healing can actually take place. It's time that we see vulnerability as one of our greatest strengths. It's time that we see emotions as tools to guide us instead of nuisances to be swept under the rug. It's time to talk about the hard stuff and learn how to support each other by holding space instead of trying to fix away our problems.

After experiencing what I've been through, I know that the heart's deepest feelings cannot be fixed. No words or actions can make that pain go away, and this is a hard reality to come to terms with as humans who want to fix. I've mentioned before that we get uncomfortable when those around us are hurting, and we don't like that feeling, so our first reaction is to do something or say something we think might help. It is my belief, however, that the greatest gift we can give ourselves and each other is to simply be present. Hold someone and allow them to cry, let them talk without responding, be present for each other. We can live in the coexistence, where movement and stillness are both equally healing.

I've also found my voice through this process. For the last couple of years, I've had a recurring dream that I'm chewing gum and I can't get it out of my mouth. I try to spit it out, and no matter how hard I try, it stays stuck. Now, I believe that this represents the search for my true, authentic voice. It's the self-expression that's been trying to come out and has finally found the courage to do so.

After almost thirty-five years of people pleasing, I'm learning that boundaries can still be compassionate. I've learned that I don't have to show up as people expect me to, and even if others are uncomfortable when I show up as "not okay," I am not obligated to take on their feelings. Part of showing up authentically in every area of my life is showing up quiet, upset, and honest about what I may be experiencing. Asking for what I need and saying no is not selfish. By expressing my feelings, I give others permission to do the same.

I also want to remember that we live in seasons. Trees are not constantly growing leaves, and we are born of that same frequency. So, maybe it's time that we remember we are not constantly meant to be growing leaves either. We are not built to be in constant production mode, and the times of resting and hibernation are crucial to thriving as living beings on the planet. The dark seasons have just as much to teach us as the light ones.

I am not the same person I was two years ago. Most of us aren't. Death is a life-altering experience for anyone connected to it. It changes the way you see the world along with almost every experience you have in it. I think differently, want different things than I used to, have different priorities, and view day-to-day living as an entirely new obstacle than I have in the past. It's truly opened my eyes and my heart to the compassion that we each need to survive this adventure we are on together—it is love and understanding we are called to share with each other.

We also can't forget to simply *live*. I've worked so hard to heal and take all of these steps to do the right things and learn the lessons, but at the end of the day, the purpose of life is joy. We don't always have to work on ourselves, and sometimes, our healing journey is simply remembering to experience life and smile. Life can and should be fun! Just last week, I woke up and decided I was tired of analyzing my process and "moving forward," so I canceled my spiritual coaching session and spent the afternoon at the pool. Letting go to live is just as important—if not more so—as doing the work.

Maybe most importantly of all, I've learned that it

takes courage to heal. It takes courage to make the choices that are right for me when it means that I might lose friendships or relationships along the way. It takes courage when people ask me what I'm doing for work and my answer is simply "resting," in a world where our value is determined by how much money we make and how productive we are. It takes courage to give up alcohol because I know it's the right choice for my body, when my peers say, "Well, you can have one drink every now and then." It takes courage to love myself for everything that I feel without self-judgments or fear of other people judging me. It takes courage to speak my truth in a world that criticizes those who fit outside the box.

And to everyone grieving and healing in any way, I see you. It takes courage to wake up every day and live in a world that looks different than we thought it would.

I do believe, however, that if we don't find the courage to heal, if we don't find the courage to use our voice and shine as the imperfect and unique souls that we came here to be, we risk losing something far greater.

I hope you find that courage, and I hope I've shown that you're not alone. I hope you come to love yourself unconditionally and know that you are worth healing. Give yourself permission to feel and be exactly who you are here and now. You are worth living a connected and joyful life, and someday, your story may inspire someone else.

Here's to our healing journey together. Here's to courage. Here's to love.

Acknowledgments

All my angels who have supported me on this journey—thank you!

Lyla, thank you for keeping me afloat in these waves.

Mandy, thank you for helping me add power to my words.

Gram and Grandad, thank you for driving to church to eat a doughnut with me. You have no idea how much I will forever appreciate that day.

To Mom and Ty, and the night we danced in the rain, singing until midnight, thank you.

Meet the Author

Dalby lives in Colorado, where she was born and raised. The beautiful Colorado weather allows her to enjoy plenty of time outside in the sunshine, which is her favorite thing to do. When she isn't writing, she's usually hiking, cycling, laughing with her friends and family, or spending time with her cat, Claire.

After working in the nonprofit world for five years, Dalby decided to change careers and become and health and fitness coach. She quickly learned that health is much more than just food and exercise, and she started to transform her coaching to include mindset and spirituality. She is passionate about empowering others to be the healthiest and most authentic versions of themselves.

Having grown up in a Science of Mind and Spirit church, she has studied and lived her spirituality for thirty years and continues to grow and learn how to help others realize their greatest potential. She is excited to see where this next chapter of her adventure takes her on the path of healing and helping others.

Meet the Coauthor

Claire rescued her mom two years ago when she fell into her lap and immediately started purring at a cat shelter. As a sassy street cat with no known history, it's hard to say how old she is, but we believe she is around ten or eleven years old.

Because she has no teeth, her tongue hangs out regularly and brings laughter to anyone who's around. She's the best cuddler you'll ever meet and never leaves her mom's side. Just like her mom, Claire loves to be outside in the sunshine. She enjoys eating flowers and chasing birds. She and Dalby often watch the sunset together on their balcony.

Claire sat in her mom's lap while her mom typed every chapter of this book. Claire can't wait for you to read it and enjoy it like she has.